ACKNOWLEDGMENTS

I would like to dedicate this book to the thousands of students who shared a classroom with me over the past 27 years. Each one touched my life in a very significant way. But there are two things in particular I learned from all of them: (1) I learned to listen with an open mind and a sensitive ear; and (2) never make a value judgment about their beliefs, opinions or lifestyles.

I would also like to thank three people in particular whose labor made my manuscript possible. Vera Sullivan, for her unselfish labor at the typewriter; Launee McKinley for making corrections and revisions; and Margaret Macaulay for her good natured encouragement and help.

"BUT TEACH, YOU AIN'T LISTENIN'"

OR

HOW TO COPE WITH VIOLENCE IN A PUBLIC SCHOOL CLASSROOM

by

Tom Yonker

Published by

R & E Publishers
P. O. Box 2008
Saratoga, California 95070

Library of Congress Card Catalog Number
82-60524

I.S.B.N.
0-88247-678-5

Copyright 1983
by
Tom Yonker

PREFACE

READERS PLEASE NOTE: The concept "unconditional love" forms the foundation for the ideas presented in this book. Simply stated, it means the ability of an individual to do things for others with no thought of being repaid — you do it simply because you want to. It also implies the ability of one to accept others simply as they are without making any value judgment about their person, their behavior or lifestyle.

One does not have to believe in a God to acknowledge the simple truth of "unconditional love;" however, the religiously inclined individual will recognize the concept as being central to the theme of the writings of the New Testament.

Application of the concept works only at a personal, one-on-one relationship. The teacher, for instance, changes the life of one student at a time and in this way he/she brings about positive behavior changes within the class.

This concept will never work in a "mass production" basis. If one hopes to bring about changes by applying the concept to large groups of people, failure will result. "Unconditional love" can only take place within the personal life of the individual. If our desire is to change the violent conditions that exist in our social order then we must first change the violent behavior that controls the lives of individuals; thus by first changing the violent behavior of individuals we change the violent conditions that are plaguing our country.

TABLE OF CONTENTS

	Page
ACKNOWLEDGMENTS	iii
PREFACE	v
INTRODUCTION	xiii

CHAPTER

I   PLEASE DON'T TELL ME TO "GO TO HELL," I HAVE BEEN THERE 1

II   OUR CULTURE REFLECTS WHAT IT VALUES — VIOLENCE IS A LEARNED BEHAVIOR 12
        Cultural Considerations: The Nature of Cooperation, Competition and Conflict in America
        Cooperation - Competition and Conflict
        Culture and the Group Process of Cooperation and Opposition (Competition)
            Culture Determines Direction and Development of Cooperation and Competition - Goal Towards Which Individuals in our Society Strive are Either Cooperative or Competitive - Primary Goal in America, Get to Top of One's Profession - Competition and Human Behavior - Cooperation and Human Behavior - American Educational Objectives - Reflection of Prevailing Social Values
        Authority and Power
            Authority - Power - Authority, Power and the Classroom Teacher
               Table 1: Implications and Possible Consequences

CHAPTER		Page
III	LOVE: IT CAN OUTLAST ANYTHING, EVEN VIOLENCE	32

    How to Get at the Causes of Violence
        Emulate the Teaching Genius of Jesus of Nazareth - Develop the Process of Moral Education
        Establishing a Criterion for Moral Behavior - Love The Specific Ingredients of the Behavior, Love - Living Example of Love Behavior, Martin Luther King's Speech - Students Have Rights, They Should be Respected - Students Should Have Input Regarding Rules That Directly Influence Their Lives - Institute Love as the Guiding Principle in the Classroom - Specific Suggestions as to How to Stop Disruptive Behavior - Specific Suggestions as to How to Minimize Disruptive Behavior
            Personal Teacher Attitudes and/or Behaviors
            Organize the Class Along Democratic Principles
            Classroom Discipline, Challenge Do Not Threaten Students
            Students Should be Treated as Unique Individuals
            Students Should be Evaluated, Not Rated

| IV | MENTAL HEALTH: ITS ROLE IN NON-VIOLENT BEHAVIOR IN SCHOOLS | 51 |

    Violence is as American As Cherry Pie
    Violence in the Schools is a Microcosm of the Revolt of Black People in American Society
    Students Want Teachers Who Believe They Can Learn and Who Teach Them, and a Curriculum That is Meaningful
        Schools Virtually Ignore The Mental Health of Their Teachers - Teacher's Problems Stem

CHAPTER		Page
IV	Continued	

        From Their Perception of Working
Conditions - Teacher Who is Sensitive
to Uniqueness of Students is Better
Equipped to Handle Fear, Frustration
and Hostility of Students - CUTE Program,
All Students were Liked, Wanted and
Accepted by the Staff - Good Teachers
Perceive Themselves in a Very Positive
Way - Teacher Earns Respect, by Accepted
and Wanting Students

    The Christian Science Monitor Study on Disruptive Students and Problems of Dyslexic Students

        Influence of Primary or Secondary Group
Relationships - Problems of Dyslexic Student
- Impressive Programs that Helped Disruptive
Students - Positive Results of Such Programs

    Problems Encountered in Getting Rid of Bad Teachers

    Traditional Method Do Not Work With Disruptive Students — Steps That Need To Be Taken

V	TEACHERS TEND TO TEACH AS THEY HAVE BEEN TAUGHT OR THE PHILOSOPHICAL BASIS OF VIOLENCE 72

    The Educational Philosophies of Essentialism and Perennialism

        Some Basic Principles - Influence on Teacher Behavior

    Five Negative Factors Which Operate in Authoritarian Classrooms — Suggested Ways to Eliminate Them

        Fear - Threat - Negative Teacher Attitudes - Bored Students - Power Struggle

    Values Clarification Materials — A Reaction to the Authoritarian Curriculum

CHAPTER		Page
V	Continued	

        Max Rafferty, the Epitomy of the Perennialist Philosophy

            The Disturbing Consequences of Rafferty's Philosophy - We Do Not Need to "Go Back To The Basics" - Teacher Should Analyze the Principles He Supports — They Will Not Help to Solve the Problems of Disruptive Behavior in Our Schools

        Student Reactions to the Authoritarian Curriculum — It is Extremely Oppressive

        An Atheistic Philosopher (Experimentalist) Confronts a Baptist Minister (Absolute Idealism); Results, Intellectual and Spiritual Growth for Both

        The Frustrations of Attempting to Develop a Consistent Philosophy of Education for a Local School District

VI   WHERE DO WE GO FROM HERE? SOME CONCLUSIONS AND RECOMMENDATIONS. . . . 116

    Conclusions

        Competitive Nature of Our Society, a Major Factor That Has Contributed to Violence in Our Schools - Clarifying Winning at the Cost of Human Values Produces Fear of Other People - The Competitive Nature of Our Society is Reflected in the Competitive Activities Employed by Classroom Teachers - Failure of Teachers to Share Their Power and Authority With Students Has Resulted in Conflict Between These Two Groups - Students Rights Have Increased in Recent Years Due to the In Loco Parentis and Due Process Legal Concepts - The Criterion of Love Can Better Cope with Classroom Violence Than the Present Authoritarian Criterion That Dominates the Public Schools

CHAPTER		Page
VI	Continued	

        - The Poor Mental Health of Teachers is a Significant Factor That Has Directly Contributed to Violence in the Classroom - Nontraditional Teaching Methods Have Been Very Successful in Combating Violence in Some of Our Schools - Getting Rid of Teachers Whose Behavior Reflects Poor Mental Health is Almost Impossible - Teachers Tend to Teach as They Have Been Taught - The Factors of Fear, Threat, Negative Teacher Attitudes, Bored Students and a Power Struggle Between Teachers and Students Have Directly Contributed to Violence in the Classroom - A Teacher's Educational Philosophy Is Going to Determine the Methods of Instruction That Are Used to Conduct Learning Activities in His/Her Classroom - Public School Administrators Spend More Time Dealing With the Symptoms Than the Causes of Violence in Our Schools - Violence is a Learned Behavior, Therefore, It Can Be Changed or Altered - The "Double Standard" Perpetuated in the Schools Has Caused Students To Lose Respect for Teachers

    Recommendations

        Administrative - Teachers - Students

BIBLIOGRAPHY 137

INTRODUCTION

Students in my Social Foundations of Education class were given the assignment of writing a paper on "The Development of a Positive Self-Concept." One of the young men wrote in his paper that "it is not easy for one to change his/her self-concept." In order for a teacher to do this, he "has to go through a new experience that helps him to perceive himself in a different way."

The ideas presented in this paper are not new; however, they are presented in the hope that they will help the reader to "perceive himself in a different way." That way, I would like to suggest, is the way of love.

Ashley Montagu, in his book, *The Humanization of Man*, revealed that ". . .love is beyond all question the most important experience in the life of a human being."[1] Research conducted by Dr. Rene Spitz in New York City tended to support Montagu's position. In her research, Dr. Spitz observed the behavior of 239 children over a two year period. These children were housed in two different homes; one was called the "Foundling Home," the other, the "Nursery." The children in the Foundling Home were not offered love (they were not held, caressed, etc.); but the nurses in the Nursery held, played with, laughed with, cuddled, etc. the children in their care. During this two year period, the emotionally starved children in the Foundling Home did not learn to speak, walk or feed themselves; also, they lost 37% of the children by death. On the other hand, Nursery was not only very successful in teaching infants these skills, but they did not lose one infant by death.[2]

Montagu insists that emotional deprivation not only severely retards the physical development of children, but the effects appear to be even more devastating upon the personality and behavior of children. "Criminal, delinquent, neurotic, psychopathic, asocial, and similar forms of behavior can, in the majority of cases, be traced to a childhood of inadequate love and emotional instability."[3]

A child constructs its picture of the world largely through experiences it has with its mother and "significant others" who are a part of its environment. If these people are loving or unloving, the child will feel that the world is loving or unloving. "When a child is not loved, it fails to learn love."[4] Such children grow up without learning the meaning of love; consequently, they enter into all kinds of shallow relationships that prove to be unfulfilling.

Show me a hardened criminal or a juvenile delinquent, Montagu contends:

> and...I will show you a person resorting to desperate means in order to attract the emotional warmth and attention he failed to get but which he so much deserves and needs. Aggressive behavior when fully understood is, in fact, nothing but love frustrated...as well as a means of taking revenge on the society which has let the person down, disillusioned, deserted, and dehumanized him. Hence the best way to approach aggressive behavior in children is not by aggressive behavior toward them but with love. And this is true not only for children but for human beings of all ages.

Montagu pointed out that the scientists of today are learning that to "live as if *life* and *love* were one is an indispensable condition," because this is the way of life which the innate nature of man demands. The idea, Montagu reminds us, is not new; but what is new is that "contemporary men should be rediscovering by scientific means, the ancient truths of the Sermon on the Mount and the Golden Rule. For human beings — and for humanity — nothing could be more important."[5]

Is there anything more important for a teacher to be doing in his/her classroom than teaching the principles of love? Most of the suggestions put forth in this paper are based, primarily, on the ethical teaching found in the Sermon on the Mount. It is hoped they will help teachers who are concerned about violence in the schools to develop their own method of dealing with the problem.

I shall pass through this world but once. If therefore, there be any kindness I can show, or any good thing I can do, let me do it now; let me not defer it or neglect it, for I shall not pass this way again.

INTRODUCTION FOOTNOTES

[1] Ashley Montagu, "The Awesome Power of Human Love," condensed from *The Humanization of Man*, reprinted in *Reader's Digest*, July, 1971, p. 103.

[2] Ibid., pp. 104-105.

[3] Ibid., pp. 104-105.

[4] Ibid., pp. 104-105.

[5] Ibid.

CHAPTER I

PLEASE DON'T TELL ME TO "GO TO HELL," I HAVE BEEN THERE

Violence had never been a part of my formative years. Love was the rule that formed the basis for all human relationships in a family of two brothers, two sisters, two parents and a grandfather. I was taught some very simple things: (1) to respect *all* of life; (2) to honor and respect my parents; (3) to respect women; (4) to honor and respect those who were older and wiser; (5) to honor and respect my country; and (6) most importantly, to love God with all my heart, mind and soul, and to love my neighbor as myself.

In 1943, as an eighteen-year-old lad who had never been away from home, I was wrenched from the protective love of a caring home and thrust, unceremoniously, into the violent world of war. I was no different than most eighteen-year-olds of that period. Most of us had a strong desire to help smash the enemy who was threatening our way of life; without question, off to war we went.

Basic training was our introduction to military life; here we learned to obey orders without question, and how to survive in hell! Hell is very real! It is a place where human behavior has gone mad; where young boys and men are not only taught to be killers, but are conditioned to believe that killing is a valid human endeavor. This hellish experience leaves its everlasting mark on every life that it touches. This is vividly illustrated in a letter I received from my father, which was delivered to me in a foxhole in France, during the Winter of 1944.

Somewhere out there among the shell holes is a hallowed spot for there is my boy. He's no exception, in fact he's just another G.I. To me, dear God, he's the answer to a prayer, that he is such a boy for my very own. I ask, dear God, that he be given strength and manhood to be an example as a soldier and as a man. In our comforts here, the foxholes seem so far away and we are free from danger; yet I am there, for there is my boy. Teach him to carry on and complete his grueling task and send him safely home, if it be Thy will, unscratched by the ravages of war. Keep his heart singing and make him big enough to overlook the faults of others. Keep him clean that he may return to his loved ones with unstained hands. Till then we dedicate him to his unfinished task that only strong men can see through to a fitting conclusion.

It matters little that my hair is a little grayer and my shoulders not so erect. I know the load is heavy for him too!

The riverlets of his mother's tears have somewhat eased her pain, but I will choke them back or hide them where none can sense my pain and loneliness. Just give him the manhood to face life's grimmest tasks and that being done, make me worthy to receive the man I sent away a boy.

I was fortunate enough to survive the "ravages of war." But my survival was not due to the "killer skills" I had been taught in basic training, but to a very simple truth I had been taught at home — "Love God with all your heart, mind and soul, and your neighbor as yourself." This simple truth helped the mind and heart of an impressionable, searching boy recognize the folly of the violence that had impregnated every fiber of his life.

Truth, at times, can be painful. I became known as the "wet-nosed kid" that should be sent back to his "mother's apron strings." I was ridiculed because I would not use foul language, tell dirty jokes, or take part in "camp orgies." But, what hurt most of all was the isolation — the isolation that almost always found me in a foxhole, alone. And yet, in spite of this treatment, my heart and mind would not let me hate those who were making life miserable for me. I did not know why I was being treated in this manner; but I knew one thing — I did not like it. And if I did not like it, did that give me the right to treat others in the same manner? I came to realize I did not have that right, but I did have the power to break this miserable circle of behavior that was aimed at me — *it could stop with me!*

As the truth of God's unconditional love for all people began unfolding within me, I found myself confronted by more confusing and frustrating situations. The Army, it is true, had trained me well. I was the best marksman in my company. I could scale a cliff and help build almost anything the Army needed to pursue the enemy. But, where were my superiors when I needed help with the problems the truth was creating for me, daily, as we marched across France and Germany:

1. I looked down the barrel of my rifle and asked myself, "Do I have the right to take the life of another human being; I thought I was taught at home to love everybody?"

2. I watched as they loaded the bodies of my buddies into trucks and carted them off like so much "cord wood," and I asked myself, "Is that all life is worth?"

3. I gazed down on the dead body of a German crewman — we shot down his plane in flames and he tried to bail out, but his "chute" did not open — and I asked myself, "He is supposed to be my enemy and I am supposed to hate him. Why?"

4. The starving children followed us across Europe and daily raided our garbage, and I asked myself, "Why do the little, innocent ones have to suffer for the mistakes of adults?"

5. I watched some of my fellow G.I.'s kill for the sake of

killing, and I asked myself, "Why do they hate so much?"

6. I watched some of my buddies get "bombed out of their skulls" and defile the female population because I was told that you had to do these things in order to be a man, and I asked myself, "If this is what it takes to be a man, then I'm not sure I want to be a man."

7. I saw women and children blown to bits as we smashed their cities into rubble, and I asked myself, "I thought we were trying to save these people from the enemy, but who is the enemy?"

8. In the hospital I would grab a buddy who was trying to climb the walls, hold him in my arms to quiet him down — the hell of war had robbed him of his senses and in his confusion and frustration all he could do was scream, strike out or sometimes cry, and I asked myself, "Why didn't somebody have the 'guts' to tell these young men that sooner or later killing becomes a very personal matter?"

9. In other wards of the hospital, I saw young men who had been blinded because they tried to drink "buzz-bomb juice" and others so messed up from V.D. that human productive life was out of the question for them, and I asked myself, "Such a waste, why?"

All of these experiences were literally tearing me apart inside. The principle of love I had been taught at home was in constant conflict with the violence that surrounded me; but all this violence had produced was the death and destruction that had been a part of my daily life for two long years. What good had it done? What permanent, loving relationships had I seen developed? What evidence could violence produce to convince me that it should be a viable part of human experience? It had produced a great deal of evidence, but all of it was destructive — it could not produce one shred of convincing evidence to persuade me that I should make violence a part of my human experience.

Most of us have been told that experience is a great teacher. As a result of my experience, the boy my father had sent off to war came home a man — a man dedicated to the truth that only through the process of love can man live an abundant life here upon this earth. As Dr. Martin Luther King, Jr. succinctly put it: "We must learn to live together as brothers or we will all perish together as fools...You develop the inner conviction that there are some things so dear...so eternally true that they are worth dying for, and if a man does not disccover something he will die for, he isn't fit to live."[1]

I believe that; do you? I believe it because my beliefs, my faith, my value system, based on the principle of love, were all tested by the most violent, hellish, destructive forces contrived by man: war. In the field of education we are fond of testing and retesting. Through this process we try to get at what is valid, what is true. The testing of my value system did not stop with the end of World War II. As the testing continued, I did two things with my value system: (1) I organized it into a consistent philosophy of life based on the ethical teachings of Jesus of Nazareth, as found in the Sermon on the Mount; and (2) I began, by word and action, to communicate this philosophy to others.

"Too soft!" "Won't work, it's too impractical," friends and colleagues kept reminding me. I. pointed out that it not only would work, but there is much historical evidence to support its effectiveness in history:

1. The Roman Empire that tried to crush the ethical teaching of Jesus has vanished from the face of the earth, but His teachings are practiced throughout the world today.

2. The social philosophy of the "Society of Friends" is based on the idea of "friendly persuasion."

3. Gandhi, through his program of non-violent, passive resistance, drove the British out of India after numerous forceful attempts had failed.

4. Dr. Martin Luther King, Jr., by applying the basic principle

of passive resistance to his movement, wrought a positive social revolution for Black folks throughout the South in the 1960's.

I found the principles of human behavior practiced by Jesus, "The Friends," Gandhi, and King, when applied consistently, not only work, but are the only principles that will work under times of stress. To illustrate, here are some examples from my own life:

I was working on a white "suburbia" playground in Oakland, California, when I received an urgent request from my supervisor asking me to take over a playground in a ghetto section of the city.
"Why me?" I asked her.
"Because, Tom," she replied, "we have not been able to keep this playground open over the past year because of constant violence and fights. The Department has tried everything it can think of and nothing has worked. We know your philosophy toward violence is different than most of ours, but we thought we would give you a crack at it."
I took the job and the playground remained open without having one fight during my tenure as the playground director.
Two incidents that took place on this playground are worth mentioning. The first one involved a group of boys who had broken into the playground and were playing a game of "hard" ball which was prohibited due to safety problems. I wasked through the gate without so much as a glance at the boys, went into my office, picked up a clipboard, shut the door, walked over to a bench where the boys were playing and sat down. As the game progressed I continued writing on some official-looking papers.
"What 'ya doin', direct," one of the boys asked.
"Just writing down some names on a report I will have to file with the Recreation Department—all directors have to do this when they have a problem on their playgrounds," I remarked.
I paid no particular attention to the game as I continued writing. In a few minutes the game broke up. Here were a gang of teen-age boys with bats and balls and all I had was a whistle. I could just see me telling them to "knock it off," or "cool it." I would have gotten my head "busted." I never did tell these young men that all I was doing was filling out

an attendance report.

The second incident involved a "mob" of teen-agers who had gathered to watch a fight a couple of blocks from the playground. It wasn't long before the mob drifted onto the playground. In the midst of the group were two Black girls who were "slugging it out." I approached the group and asked them to take their fight back to where it had started, which was anywhere but the playground as far as I was concerned. Nothing happened! I stepped up behind one of the girls and pinned her arms against her side—this, I quickly realized, was a big mistake. The attention of the "mob" had been directed at the two girls. The minute I touched the Black girl (I was the only white person present), all eyes were focused on me. I turned her loose in a hurry and said to the group: "We do not permit fights on this playground. I would appreciate it if you would step outside the fence and, if you want to continue to 'beat each other to a pulp, be my guest.'"

I turned my back on the "mob" and started walking away. At that moment I experienced the greatest fear of my life. I had no idea what that "mob" would do. For a few moments there was a deathly silence. Then one of the spectators said to the two girls: "Come on. Let's go out on the sidewalk and finish this."

I just kept walking away as the crowd turned and went out the gate.

Why didn't they "jump" me? I was an intruder on their "turf;" I was not "one of them." There was nothing to stop them. Or was there?

A number of the young people in that "mob" were kids who were regular visitors to the playground. They had enjoyed the benefits of a lively recreation program with the knowledge that no one was going to "smash them in the face." They also were very much aware of my attitude toward fighting—this attitude had been the driving force behind giving back to them their playground. It had been over a year since the playground had been open—constant violence had kept it closed before that. If violence erupted again they knew the playground would be closed immediately.

I cite these two examples for a very specific reason. The young people who lived in the general area learned to survive by the "law of the jungle." That law was founded upon the principles of force and violence. Oh, they knew how to enforce this law and anyone who got in their way soon paid the price.

I didn't like their rules, simply because I did not know how to use force in accomplishing my goals. So, instead of meeting their anger, force and violence with like behavior, I employed the principle of love—I may not like the act you are directing at me, but I still love you.

My approach, at first, confused and frustrated these young people. They knew how to react to force; "Man, you hit me and I'll hit you one better." "But," they would say to themselves, "what do I do with this guy. I swear at him; I throw things at him and even take a poke at him and all he does is grin at me and suggest that we play a friendly game of this or that."

I consistently used the principle of love, and within a short time I had won the respect of most young people who visited the playground. That respect, I am sure, is the one thing that kept me from getting my "head beat in" the afternoon I was confronted by the "mob" that was "egging" on the fight between the two Black girls.

A few years later I moved on to Durham, North Carolina to attend Duke University. While attending graduate school, I also served as the director for a community center in an all-white suburb. My task was to develop recreational activities for all age levels. One activity I developed was a "Pop Warner" football team for boys ages eight through twelve. We were the "new kid on the block" in the local age-group football program. Most of the opposing coaches, and some of my colleagues in the Recreation Department, reminded me that my attitude toward coaching would end up getting us "killed" by the other teams. I don't know if we got "killed," but I do know that we ended up winning the league championship.

None of the members of our team, including the coach, had ever been involved in a football program. Together we established the rules that governed our program. These rules could be summed up in this statement: "It's not whether we win or lose that counts, but how we play the game."

Four different incidents from my high school teaching days remind me that love, tempered with a sense of humor, can do much to thwart disruptive behavior in the classroom. The first incident took place my very first day of teaching. I was standing at the blackboard writing, when, whack! Someone had thrown an eraser at me and it hit the blackboard with a crack. The noise sent me about two feet in the air which, no doubt, gave rise to the laughter from the students. Without turning around, I gained my composure and went right on writing. I finished my work, stooped over, picked up the eraser and said to the class: "I don't know who threw the eraser, but whoever did can never play on my baseball team if their aim is that bad." To this day, I still do not know who hurled that object!!

A couple of months later the next incident occurred. It involved a big, handsome, freshman football player and an art teacher. It seems that both of these individuals came to the high school at the same time. While attending junior high, the student had had some problems with this teacher. Now she was "riding" him again for no apparent reason—he did not have her for a class. On the day in question, he came barging into my classroom, during lunch, in a fit of rage. He literally screamed at me: "If that old bag doesn't get off my back, I'm going to punch her out!" I tried to calm him down, but he would have none of that. Finally I said to him: "Why don't you hit me? If you don't, you are going to hit someone else that is not too sympathetic and you'll really get yourself in a jam."

"I can't do that, Mr. Yonker—I can't hit someone that cares about me!" He hardly got the words out of his mouth when he swung around and put his fist through one of my cupboard doors. He pulled his fist out of the splintered door and sheepishly looked at me.

"I'm sorry, Mr. Yonker. I didn't mean to mess up your room, but I sure feel better—for that I want to thank you."

"Don't mention it," I replied, and he turned and walked out of my room.

The incidents mentioned here took place in 1955 during my first year of teaching. Four years later, two incidents occurred in my senior problems class that are worth mentioning. The first happened during a class discussion on "Family Living." I was talking to the class about the concept of "honoring your mother and father." Without warning, a male student sitting in the back of the class rose to his feet and blurted out: "I should honor that no-good, dirty, blankety-blank, s.o.b., old man of mine. Why?"

In shocked disbelief, I just stood and stared at him and the class sat in stunned silence during his short tirade about his father. When he finished he sat down and I jolted myself back to the reality of dealing with this uncomfortable outburst. After a brief silence I regained my composure and said to the class:

"Apparently, John disagrees with what I was saying. Do you think the point of view he expressed about his father is justified? Instead of giving you my reaction, I would be more interested in what the rest of you think. Please break up into your small discussion groups and analyze John's remarks."

As a result of this exercise, the class formulated two conclusions: (1) based on what they personally knew about the man known as John's father, there was little evidence that John should honor this man as father; and (2) the class wanted John to know that not all fathers were like his, nor did he or any other male have to be that kind of father.

Why didn't I tell John to sit down and be quiet, or just "kick" him out of class? This would have been the reaction of most teachers. If I had done that, one of two things would have happened: (1) he would have become more frustrated and angry if I had told him to "shut up;" or, (2) if I had "kicked" him out of class, he would have left with the mistaken notion that he, and his classmates, thought all fathers were like his father, "rotten to the core."

THANK YOU, JOHN, FOR TEACHING ME HOW TO *LISTEN!* It turned out to be a tremendous learning experience for all of us who were part of that senior problems class.

This class incident with John was, to say the least, a most traumatic event. But not all memorable classroom events have to be of this nature in order for learning to take place. In fact, John Dewey reminds all teachers that, "to ignore what is thus being learned will not prevent the learning." In other words, students in our classes are learning a lot more than what is apparent to most teachers. This fact was brought to my attention in a very positive way through a very inconspicuous encounter with a classmate of John's. I had made a number of "one-liner" signs and hung them up around the room. I tacked one over the door so that all students, as they left the class could not miss it. It read, "Love Your Enemies." On this particular day, the bell rang and the students filed out, with one exception. Steve stopped at my desk, looked me straight in the eye and remarked: "Mr. Yonker, if I loved everybody, I wouldn't have any enemies would I?" In amazement, I just stared at the back of Steve's head as he walked out the door.

CHAPTER FOOTNOTES

[1]Martin Luther King, Jr., from an address delivered before the Episcopal Society for Cultural and Facial Unity at the Episcopal Church's General Convention in St. Louis, Missouri, 1964.

CHAPTER II

OUR CULTURE REFLECTS WHAT IT VALUES — VIOLENCE IS A LEARNED BEHAVIOR

Violence is a learned behavior — thus a behavior that is learned can be changed and/or altered. But, if a behavior is going to be changed, one must get at the root (cause) of the behavior. Treating the symptoms of the behavior, and in this case, violent behavior, will do little if anything to reduce violence in the public schools.

There are many professionals in the field of education who would have us believe that it is "human nature" to be violent. That, by nature, man is a violent creature, therefore, the best we can hope for is to "keep in check," or curb his violent tendencies. If, in point of fact, this is true, then how do we, as educators, explain away the Tasaday people of the Philippine Islands? This small group of people have no word in their vocabulary for war or violence and they possess no weapons. They have not learned the meaning of the terms, "war," "violence," "hate," "weapon," "destroy." They have not made these terms part of their vocabulary, nor given expression to them by means of hostile behavior, because they are not part of their culture.

The primary function of education within a culture is not merely the impartation of information; it is the molding of the character and personality of the young — the process through which children and youth acquire the motives, attitudes, knowledge, skills, and the ways in which they live. Only in this way can a society assure itself of the "reproduction of type" from generation to generation through education of the young. *In this sense, cultural reproduction is as essential to society as biological reproduction.* The basic function of society does not vary from society to society. What does vary is *the type of social order to be maintained.* Thus, in every land, the school undertakes to mold a specific kind of character and personality which is *able* and *willing* to function effectively in the life of the society served by the school.

Hence, education is ultimately a MORAL and POLITICAL, as well as an INTELLECTUAL affair. In the last analysis, the *authority of the teacher* rests on the basic intellectual and moral commitments of the society served by the school. On this ground, the educational profession may be justified in opposing and resisting demands which violate these commitments, even though, for the moment, the demands appear to be supported by the majority of the people in the community. When the educational profession does this it is saying that, in its judgment, the DEMOCRATIC TRADITION EMBODYING THE DEEPEST INTELLECTUAL AND MORAL COMMITMENTS OF THE AMERICAN PEOPLE have been violated, and what is needed is reevaluation of what is *most* valued in our society.

A good illustration of this has been the move, in recent years, through Title VI and Title IX, to break down the barriers of all sorts of discrimination that have been going on for years in the public schools. If this were not true, then why the need for laws and statutes on discrimination? The issue here is not discrimination but what *is most valued in our society.* To identify THE value or even a list of values that would be universally acceptable in our pluralistic society would be most foolhardy; however, group life is a fundamental fact of American life and within this lifestyle there are two basic processes of group life at work—cooperation and opposition—that have helped to produce conflicting values within our culture.

There are a number of questions which arise when cooperation and opposition are considered. Why is it that cooperation and opposition are not everywhere the same? Why are some cultures more cooperative than others; or why are some more competitive than others? But whatever the question, there are clearly cultural considerations that help determine how the social processes—cooperation or opposition—operate in a given society.

To ignore these cultural considerations does not mean they do not exist. And for too many years educators have ignored, consciously or unconsciously, some basic cultural phenomena that have tended to breed violence within our culture. Ignorance of this fact has resulted in piecemeal attempts to cope with the *symptoms* of violence while the *causes* of violence within public education have been virtually ignored.

I. **CULTURAL CONSIDERATIONS:**[1] The Nature of Cooperation, Competition and Conflict in America.

    A.   Cooperation:
           1.   The social process takes its form of cooperation when individuals all do essentially the same thing in order to achieve a common goal.
           2.   The study of cooperation by social thinkers has been slighted, largely due to the phenomena of opposition which is reflected in our highly competitive society.
           3.   Also, there is a tendency to approach the study of cooperation as an indirect study of conflict (example: marital adjustments are inferred from a study of marital maladjustments) — social scholars tend to be competition-conscious.

    B.   Competition and Conflict:
           1.   Competition is the most fundamental form of social struggle within our culture. It occurs where there is an insufficient supply of anything that human beings desire within a specific social context.
           2.   Rivalry is a *personalized* form of competition. Under these conditions competition tends to become more *keen* which can easily lead to hostility between the competitors. As a result *antagonistic competition* or *social conflict* may develop.
           3.   The idea that struggle is all-important was supported by Darwin's doctrine of natural selection (survival of the fittest), and this generalization has been advanced and supported by numerous social thinkers

of the 19th and 20th centuries. The concept, however, was overplayed by Darwin, while neglecting the fact that cooperation plays a major role in survival.
4. Conflict itself may involve cooperation. Example: the individual members of a football team must cooperate on the field of conflict in order to win the game.
5. Competition as a condition of cooperation: Example: during World War II, war plants competed against each other to see which plant could produce the most, but the competition resulted in the cooperative well-being of the entire nation.
6. Rivalry is evident in children at age three; by age six it has developed so rapidly that it is generally characteristic of children in our culture.
7. Studies show that competition between groups, or individuals, brings forth greater effort than does work lacking the competitive elements[2] — it furnishes motivation in the desire to excel, obtain recognition, or to win an award.

II. **CULTURE AND THE GROUP PROCESSES OF COOPERATION AND OPPOSITION** (Competition)

A. Culture determines both the direction and the development of cooperation and competition—these processes are subject to many pressures and controls; consequently, the competitive and cooperative behavior of individuals varies from culture to culture.

B. The primary goal toward which individuals in a society strive are either cooperative or competitive. Consequently, it is possible in all societies to characterize a given people as primarily cooperative or competitive, depending on the *activity they value most*.

C. In America, the primary goal is to get to the top of one's chosen profession. Progress toward this goal is generally measured by the amount of money one earns. Consequently, the American idea of success is individualistic.

> "Modern culture is economically based on the principle of individual competition ...From its economic center, competition radiates into all other activities and permeates love, social relations, play. Therefore, competition is a problem for everyone in our culture."[3]

D. Competition and human behavior.
1. In America, children from the cradle are so conditioned to our highly competitive culture that we regard competitive behavior as only natural and proper within our society.
2. Most Americans cannot see how cooperation can be as effective a motive as competition.
3. In competition, the drive is "will to win" or a desire for recognition.
4. In our society, there is a close relationship between competition and security — people compete to obtain *immediate* security to protect against insecurity in the future.
5. Competition gives expression to the desire for new experience.
6. Competition permits one person to feel superior to another.

E. Cooperation and human behavior.
1. Cooperation with others to achieve a common goal is a very satisfying behavior in our culture.
2. Recognition is always in terms of group values; that is, in a cooperative society, the desire for recognition will best be satisfied by those who cooperate

best.
3. The drive for security is more likely to be satisfied in a cooperative than in a competitive society, because of the protection a group supplies within a cooperative society.
4. An individual within a cooperative society is protected a good deal more against the humiliation of defeat; striving to "get past" others, as in our society, may bring glory, but more often than not, it can lead to failure.
5. A desire for affection can be better satisfied in a cooperative than a competitive society—people like it better when we work with them and for them than they do when we surpass them in competition.

In summary, a cooperative society caters largely to the *security* and *response* wishes of individuals, while a competitive society gives more response to the desire for new experiences and personal recognition.

F. American educational objectives — a reflection of prevailing *social values*. One of the best ways to discover the goals in a society is to examine the structure of its institution of education. The group is always interested in transmitting its goals to the young in order to guarantee survival of the group standards. The surest way to accomplish this within any society is for the group in power to win over the young and this is best accomplished within the educational organization of the society. In America, when one examines the school system, it is seen at once to reflect the competitive spirit of the culture:
1. In general, the better students do not help those that are deficient, but rather depend upon the inferiority of the others.
2. As in the larger society, there is intense competition for grades and, if possible, the winning of honors.
3. The tremendous growth and expenditure of monies for competitive athletics within our schools.

4. The tendency for school districts to hire classroom teachers who can also coach athletics, even though more qualified classroom teachers are available.
5. There are numerous studies which show that our culture, operating in part through the schools, builds up an intensive competitive spirit in the young.[4]
6. These studies also indicate that cooperation is easier than in a heterogeneous society like ours.
7. Open conflict with our culture is supported by the traditions of democracy. In other words, where people are allowed the freedom to speak out, to think for themselves, the chances for open conflict are greater than where such privileges are denied — a good example was the open rebellion of high school and college age youth during the 1960's.

III. AUTHORITY AND POWER

A. Authority

By definition authority implies that '...a person or body...' is impowered with the '...right to control, command or determine...' It further implies the power to '...direct the actions or thoughts of others.' This power is derived from the person's 'station' or 'rank' and permits the person to exercise authority over subordinates. The exercise of this authority may operate unconsciously or through persuasion.[5]

B. Power

The concept power, when exercised by an individual, implies that he/she 'possesses control or command over others;' it also implies 'delegating authority' which is vested in a person or persons in a particular capacity.[6]

C. Authority, Power and the Classroom Teacher. The concepts *authority* and *power*, when applied to public school administrators and teachers imply some very specific things which can have very specific consequences for students. The implications and possible consequences are shown in Table 1.

TABLE 1

	Implication		Possible Consequences
1.	Impowered — the teachers have certain powers granted to them by the board of education, statutes of the state and federal government.	1.	Students, in general, until very recently (due to court decision), have not possessed such power.
2.	Right to control command determine: administrators and teachers have been granted certain specific rights by legislation and the courts to control (1) selection of teaching staff; (2) selection of curricular offerings and related materials; (3) methods of instruction; (4) student behavior; (5) student activities; and (6) the testing and counseling of students.	2.	In general, no such rights have been granted to students. Even in areas of student behavior, the courts in Gordon vs. Oak Park School District No. 97, 24 Ill. App 3d 131. 320 N.E. 2d 389 (1974), "recognized that within the broad delegation of parental authority a teacher has the right to verbally chastise a pupil." Even though the teacher intentionally "humiliated, degraded and shamed (a student) with disparaging

TABLE 1 (Continued)

Implications	Possible Consequences
	2. (continued) remarks," the teacher will not be held liable without proof of wantonness or malice." It is significant to note here that virtually every form of pupil discipline — including corporal punishment — is legally permissible with that qualification.[7]
3. Power to direct the action and thoughts of others. Teachers are granted the power to "direct the actions and thoughts of students." Misuse of this power led to a method of learning (indoctrination) that proceeds namely in one direction: from "communicator" to "communicatee." This leads the proponents (teachers) to belieeve that their position is so "supremely true or good. . .as to eliminate the need for critical, scrupulous, thoroughgoing comparison with other doctrines."[9] This leads to the conclusion that: "most ways of learning that have been	3. This power is not granted to students; however, by law, the first and fourteenth amendments of The Constitution do protect a student's right to freedom of expression, and the courts have protected their right in the case of Scoville vs. Board of Education of Joliet Township High School District 204! — The decision of the United States Court of Appeals.[8] Theordore Brameld also points out the necessity for ". . .academic freedom as the right of children and adults to confront any controversial issue of any importance."[10] It implies un-

TABLE 1 (Continued)

Implications	Possible Consequences
3. (continued) and still are protected in the name of education are largely or wholly indoctrinated."[11]	3. (continued) restricted opportunity to examine facts and test hypotheses. "But the choice that results from intelligent activity are still not to be indoctrinated — that is, they must not be taught so as to preclude questioning or possible alternatives."[12]
4. Power is "derived from the person's rank and permits the person (teacher and/or administrator) to exercise authority over *subordinates*." The statement above makes one fact absolutely clear, namely, that someone (the teacher) is in a superior position, and someone (the student) is in an inferior position. And the criteria used to support the superior position of the teacher is his/her 'rank.' Rank, in general, is based on two considerations: (1) the fact that the teacher is an adult; and (2) the fact that the teacher has been through a training exper-	4. The student is "powerless" when discussing 'rank,' and the positions of superior/inferior for the following reasons. In our culture, the 'rank' of adult, due to experience, education, knowledge, understanding, etc., grants adults the right to exercise (our laws tend to support this claim) control over the children and youth of our land. Since the mores of the culture and the laws of the land tend to grant a great deal of power to the 'rank' of adult, most adults are fully aware that they can, and do, exercise a great deal of authority over the child

TABLE 1 (Continued)

Implications	Possible Consequences
4. (continued) (teacher training program) that is superior to that possessed by the student.	4. (continued) and youth population. The *exercise* of this power is a *fact* of life in our culture; unfortunately, we cannot assume that simply because an adult is granted such power, he/she will exercise it with skill, understanding, equity, fairness and justice when dealing with children and youth. The person's power, as derived from his 'rank,' automatically sets up a confrontation relationship of superior (teacher) vs. inferior (student). Consequently, teachers frequently use the phrase "they (students) are on one side and we (teachers) are on the other." One teacher, Jenny Gray, even wrote a book describing this relationship, *The Teacher's Survival Guide: How to Teach Teen-Agers and Live to Tell About It.*[13] She points out that *control* is necessary if *learning* is to take place, and once a teacher signs a contract that teacher is obligated to be

TABLE 1 (Continued)

Implications	Possible Consequences
	4. (continued) governed by duly elected persons (adults). This, she points out is the way our society can function in an orderly way and keep our young people from becoming "adept at the fine art of insurrection."[14] Control is a necessary ingredient of learning; but Jenny Gray implies throughout her book that control should be exercised solely by the teacher. Question. If external controls imposed by the teacher have not worked in the past (violence in the schools is on the increase), how can it possibly work in the future? An alternative is suggested; students need to learn how to develop an internalized system of self-control, which will help them become responsible for their own behavior.
5. The exercise of this authority may "operate unconsciously or through persuasion." A teacher's age, experience, educational	5. The implication of this position is best summarized in a statement made by John Dewey: "Pupils learn from him (the teacher) to

TABLE 1 (Continued)

Implications	Possible Consequences
5. (continued) background, even voice or size, etc., might threaten or intimidate *unconsciously* his/her students. Example: "Students, you will call me Mr. Jones;" "You will address me as Dr. Smith;" or, "I'm older than you are, therefore, I know what's right for you."	5. (continued) value certain things and to disregard others...He influences their personality, their outlook on life...It is essential for teachers to think in these terms and to keep in mind that pupils are constantly learning for good, or ill, along all these lines. To ignore what is thus being learned will not prevent the learning...The teacher has accordingly an obligation to examine his philosophy, to be aware that he does affect others, and to build for himself an *examined, critically chosen* set of values, rather than to act *haphazardly* and *unconsciously*.[15]

End of Table 1

According to Arthur Combs, a teacher has two kinds of authority. One is "unearned" authority; the other is "earned."[16] A teacher's "unearned" authority comes with his/her teaching assignment—he/she is the assigned "boss" of the class. The teacher may have the reputation of being a "fair" teacher, but neither the power vested in him/her by the role of teacher, nor an excellent reputation, will authomatically result in genuine communication between teacher and student. "Such authority," Combs pointed out, "increases in direct proportion to the degree of 'earned' authority—the authority the students themselves invest in the teacher as a result of their personal discovery of who this teacher is, what he believes, and stands for, and how he operates."[17] That is why it is imperative that every teacher examine his/her philosophy of education, be aware that he/she does directly affect the lives of students, and build for himself/herself an examined, critically chosen set of values.

Traditionally, teachers have exercised a great deal of authority and power over the lives of students who attended public schools. In early American public schools, the teacher's authority was absolute. In the late 1800's the legal doctrine of *in loco parentis* attempted to limit a teacher's authority to the disciplining of students.[18] This concept can be traced to Blackstone's Commentaries:

> A parent may also delegate part of his parental authority ...to the tutor or schoolmaster of his child; who is then *in loco parentis*, and has such a portion of the power of the parent, viz. that the restraint and correction, as may be necessary to answer the purpose for which he is employed.[19]

Interpretation of this principle by school authorities has not been consistent. Some educators used this principle to permit the schools to exercise almost absolute authority over the students who attended their schools. Bolmeier pointed out, however, the phrase, "as may be necessary to answer the purpose for which he is employed," implied that the doctrine of *in loco parentis* never authorized school authorities to completely displace parental authority in all matters relating to the school.[20]

The *limited* scope of the doctrine, Bolmeier emphasized, "...is frequently violated by broadening the scope of the teacher's authority and responsibility beyond that of maintaining discipline."[21] Disregard for this limitation is cause for much of the litigation brought against public schools over the past twenty-five years.[22]

The *due process* doctrine and the rights of students raised many questions during the 1960's, regarding procedures used by some school authorities when administering disciplinary practices. In the 1967 precedental Gault Case, the United States Supreme Court found that before a juvenile can be found guilty and penalized he must be accorded the same due process rights accorded adults:

(1) notice of the charges;
(2) right to counsel;
(3) right to confrontation and cross-examination of the witness;
(4) privilege against self-incrimination;
(5) right to transcript of the proceedings; and
(6) right to appellate review.[23]

The term "due process" stems from the Fifth and Fourteenth Amendments of the United States Constitution. Both of these amendments state, in essence, that no citizen of the United States of America shall be deprived ". . .of life, liberty or property, without due process of law. . ."

A study of the United States Constitution is a required part of the high school curriculum in the State of California. In 1968, I was teaching this as part of the curriculum in the junior year American history class, when suddenly one of the students asked: "Do these laws we have been talking about apply to me?" I replied: "Are you a citizen of the United States?" "Yes," the girl answered. "Then these laws," I pointed out, "would apply to you the same as they would to any adult citizen of our country."

"Do you mean," she continued, "that I have the same rights regarding these laws as adults?"

"Why don't you do some investigating on your own?" I suggested.

This was the beginning of one of the most exciting learning experiences I have ever encountered in a classroom. The entire class decided that they wanted to be a part of this investigation. The class wanted to find out a specific thing, namely: since the Constitution is the supreme law of the land, and since all citizens and people living in this country are obligated to obey it, then, in a school setting, do the laws apply to both school officials and students? The students in my class were asking this question because they felt student government, and the Constitution, in their school was a "farce" — they were a farce because students felt powerless to make changes. If the students made a suggestion that was unpopular with the administration, the principal would veto it and replace it with one of his own.

In order for the class to carry out its investigation, students were divided into six groups. Each group wrote to a different school in a state other than California. The materials they received were discussed and analyzed by the entire class — the class came to the following conclusion. Some public school officials respected the rights of their high school students and granted them the privilege to exercise some authority in the governing of student activities. Why, the students in my class asked, were they being denied these same rights and privileges? I suggested that they take their concern to the principal.

During the first part of the first meeting, the principal was most cordial; but when he realized the nature of the students' concern, he conveniently found reasons to avoid these students when they tried to meet with him on several other occasions.

The students' concern was valid. The principal had formed a committee to study student government, but he never once called this group together during the year. Students in my class wanted to know why. The principal gave them no answer.

The morning of the student body elections, an assembly was held in order to introduce all candidates to the entire student body. Students from my American History class, through planned strategy, persuaded the candidates to hold off the election, temporarily. Immediately following the assembly, the principal circulated a memo to all classes: "Following the last class of the day, the committee to study student government will meet in room 105, the large assembly room." The ten members of the committee (five students and five teachers) showed up as well as the principal and two hundred students. For the first time during the school year the principal *listened* to what students had to say. Why does it take a crisis before those in a position of power will listen?

Actually, the answer is quite simple! Authority figures who react this way are very easily threatened by individuals, or groups, who would question their authority. Then why not avoid situations that result in such confrontations!

One of the best ways to do this is to invite all parties concerned to *share* in the responsibility of exercising authority. In order for a teacher, principal or any school official to be able to do this, he/she must feel secure within him/herself. If the teacher does feel secure, then he/she knows that, no matter what happens in his/her class, the situation will not become threatening to anyone, because both the students and the teacher will have an opportunity to help determine the outcome. Through the process of "give and take" a mutual plan of action will emerge, thus giving all parties—particularly students—the feeling that, "we had a hand in the formation of the plan."

The advantages of teachers sharing their power and authority outweigh the disadvantages:

1. Students feel they have a "stake" in what is going on in the classroom, therefore, they are not going to disrupt the classroom by engaging in negative behaviors.
2. Teachers will *earn* the respect of their students.
3. An atmosphere of *trust* will become a part of the classroom.
4. Students will develop more responsible behavior because they will be given an opportunity to act responsibly—young people learn by doing.

John Dewey clarified this axiom when he pointed out that pupils learn from the teacher to value certain things and to reject others. The teacher influences the students' personalities and their outlook on life; and furthermore, Dewey reminds teachers that pupils are constantly learning both good and ill from the example set by the teacher in the classroom. Consequently, for the teacher "to ignore what is thus being learned will not prevent the learning."[24]

A vivid illustration of this fact emerges from the following dialogue between an instructor working in a teacher-training program and his students. The discussion centered around a teacher who hit the hands of her pupils with a ruler if they failed to make the correct response to her questions.

Instructor: How much teaching really gets done when you use force or threaten a child?

Jamie: It teaches force...Violence breeds violence. If you use force with children...maybe you are teaching them that force is the best way for them to get what

Instructor: they want. But what is it that children learn when someone convinces by force?
Tom: They learn that this is the only way to convince somebody to learn something.
Instructor: Well, suppose some of the teachers use force and you learn that lesson. In addition...what have you learned?
Tom: I've learned how to apply force, how to use it... Also, I have learned how to hate the person that applied the force.
Brenda: Only the strongest person wins!
Instructor: That's right! That I'm stronger and bigger than you are...have more weapons that you have, I can terrorize you. Being bigger, stronger, hitting harder, hurting more is effective. *That's really the lesson you teach.*[25]

What then is the lesson that each teacher in a public school classroom is trying to teach? Every teacher who really cares about the welfare of children and youth will ask himself/herself this question: "If my words and actions portray anger and violence, am I setting a bad example and/or teaching my students how to be hateful and violent? On the other hand, if I treat my students with respect, love, understanding and forgiveness, is there a good chance my students' behavior will be more productive than violent?" A teacher will get back from the students the "measure" that has been given to them!

CHAPTER FOOTNOTES

[1]Most of the ideas in this section were borrowed from William F. Ogburn/Meyer F. Nimkoff, *Sociology*, Houghton Mifflin Co., 1946, pp. 344-391.

[2]Ibid., p. 353.

[3] Ibid., p. 359.

[4] Ibid., p. 360.

[5] Lawrence L. Barnhart (Ed.), *The American College Dictionary*. Harper Bros., 1950, p. 84.

[6] Ibid., p. 950.

[7] Edward C. Bolmier, *Legality of Student Disciplinary Practices*, The Michie Company, 1976, p. 149.

[8] Ibid., p. 87-89.

[9] Theodore Brameld, *Patterns of Educational Philosophy: Divergence and Convergence in Culturalogical Perspective*, Holt, Rinehart and Winston, Inc., 1971, p. 193.

[10] Ibid.

[11] Ibid, pp. 469-470.

[12] Ibid., p. 193.

[13] Jenny Gray, *The Teacher's Survival Guide*. Fearon Publishers, 1967.

[14] Ibid., p. 1.

[15] John Dewey, as quoted in *Elementary School Principal*, Sept. 1947, p. 46.

[16] Arthur Combs and others. *The Professional Education of Teachers* (Second Edition). Allyn Bacon and Co., Inc., p. 81.

[17] Ibid.

[18] Edward C. Bolmeier. *Judicial Excerpts Governing Students and Teachers*. The Michie Co., 1977, p. 115.

[19] Ibid.

[20] Ibid.

[21] Ibid., p. 116.

[22] Ibid., pp. 115-119.

[23] Ibid., p. 123.

[24] Dewey, as found in *Elementary School Principal*, Sept. 1947, p. 46.

[25] *Now I Have Known Me*, Report on Mental Health of Cooperative Urban Teacher Education Program. Mid-Continent Regional Educational Laboratory, Kansas City, Missouri, Spring, 1970, Volume 1, Number 4, pp. 49-51.

CHAPTER III

LOVE: IT CAN OUTLAST ANYTHING, EVEN VIOLENCE

Violence is a fact of life in our public schools. What are some of the factors in our society and our public schools that have helped to produce this type of behavior? Here are a few:

1. Stress placed on *competition* in all areas of both social and school life.
2. The misuse and misunderstanding of the concepts of *power* and *authority* by individuals in positions of responsibility.
3. The attitude among some teachers and administrators that permits the concept of superior/inferior to perpetuate itself within the context of the school curriculum.
4. The claim made by some educators that the aim of education, in a time of rapid social change, is to remain neutral (when confronted with controversial social issues), and/or to help students acquire knowledge.
5. Perpetuation of the concept that to be violent is only a part of human nature.
6. The willingness of educators to deal with the *symptoms* of violence, but their unwillingness (or inability) to deal with the *causes* of violence within our schools.

Most of the approaches used to attack the problem of violence in our public schools have done little, if anything, to deal directly with the six factors mentioned on the previous page. That is why I ask the question,

"Do we really want to solve the problem of violence that is presently plaguing our public schools?" Silly question! That's like asking, "Do we want to get rid of cancer?" Of course we do. There is one major difference. Doctors are presently analyzing all possible data that might be related to the *causes* of cancer. In the field of education, when the problem of violence is discussed, the topic usually centers around the *symptoms* of violence and not the root causes.

To get at the causes of violence in public schools, those concerned about the problem must do at least two things: (1) *work* — take the time and effort to read, discuss, and research materials that contain information about the *basic nature of our culture* — this should help the individual develop an *awareness* of the strengths and weaknesses of our social system; and (2) *take a chance* — use the information to develop specific guidelines that could help to change the attitudes and behavior patterns of children and youth within our culture — only in this way can anything be done about the problem of violence in our public schools.

A culture reflects what it values, and apparently our culture values attitudes and behaviors that produce violent behavior in people. Can these values by changed? There are those in the field of education (presently they are in the majority) who say it is not the school's position to take the lead in bringing about social change. The school cannot create. It cannot generate new social ideas. It can only reflect or transmit those ideas and values which are socially acceptable. In social ideas — in this case violence — the school can rise no higher than the source of the thoughts, feelings and beliefs of the dominant groups in the society in which it finds itself. Educators who advocate such a position point out that the social obligation of the teacher is one, or all, of the following: (1) to guard or promote the most permanent interest of society; (2) remain neutral in times of social change; (3) to train the minds of children and to help them acquire knowledge; or (4) to provide insight only as to the direction of social change, but not to provide measures needed for the building of a new social order.

In 1929, a university president wrote an article for the July 10th issue of the *New York Times*. He was intrigued by the references that were made about the man, Jesus of Nazareth, as a teacher. If Jesus was a teacher extraordinary, he asked, what were the essentials of his teaching genius?

1. He was not interested in giving his hearers new information. He was interested in giving them a *new way of looking at all information*, old and new.
2. He was not interested in having his hearers absorb a mass of standardized information, but in having them think about the *pressing problems of their own lives*.
3. He was not interested in increasing their knowledge. He was interested in *increasing their understanding*.
4. He was not concerned to have them practice in remembering. He wanted them to *practice thinking*.

The writer of this article closed his remarks by pointing out that Jesus, the man, would have a most difficult time getting a job in any of our educational institutions, and yet, he pointed out, he was one of the great teachers of his day.

He would have the same problem today! Why? He advocates four things that schools could do to help us change our attitudes and behavior, but these four things do not *reflect* the *majority* position of the teaching profession: (1) all information should be approached with an open mind; (2) information, to be relevant, should help students solve the pressing problems of their own lives; (3) increasing students' *understanding* is far more important than increasing their knowledge; and (4) the process of relevant education should be to *practice* thinking, not memorizing facts.

The approach suggested here can help students deal with rapid social change — would anyone doubt that we are now in a period of rapid social change? One of the results of this change has been the growing violent behavior in our public schools.

The overriding issue for the schools is simply, what role are they going to play in this era of social change? Are they going to merely reflect what is going on in this society? Are they going to promote the general welfare of the state? Are they going to remain neutral or passive in dealing with social change and just concentrate on training young minds and disseminating knowledge?

Obviously, these approaches have failed miserably in trying to deal with violence in the public schools. Then *who*, or *what* (group, institution, etc.) shall select the issues to be taught and determine the direction education shall take in our public schools?

To ponder this question, one must accept the fact that moral education is one of the primary issues in our society. John Dewey very pointedly emphasized that moral education is a problem of securing knowledge and connecting that knowledge with the habits and inclinations of students with the subject matter acquired in any course of study which builds social interest and develops the intelligence needed to make that interest effective in practice (conduct) is helping the student develop moral insight. Out of this process emerges the necessary moral traits which a democratic culture badly needs — open-mindedness, sincerity, breadth of outlook, thoroughness and the assuming of responsibility for ideas put forth by the individual, as well as his/her actions. Authoritarian practices found in so many schools, Dewey pointed out, reduce morals to a set of stagnant codes or rules that become a machine-like routine instead of enlightening the consciousness of man.

Dewey's concept of moral education intrigued me as a first-year teacher back in 1955. I developed guidelines in my classroom for the implementation of his ideas. Before long I found myself in conflict with some of my administrators. In an attempt to support my position, I shared with my principal the following excerpt from a document put out by the Educational Policies Commission of the N.E.A.:

> The development of moral and spiritual values is basic to *all* other educational objectives. Education uninspired by moral and spiritual values is directionless. Values unapplied in human behavior are empty.
>
> Again, some teachers may become so completely engrossed in the task of teaching (subject matter). . .that the moral and spiritual implications of their work escape adequate attention. Having a natural and proper respect for their particular subject matter, they may devote all their strength to the tasks of 'covering' the material. . . success in mastering the various subjects of study need not conflict with the development of moral and spiritual values. Nevertheless, if any conflict does arise between these two purposes, there must be no questions whatever as to the willingness of the school to subordinate *all other*

considerations to those which concern moral and spiritual standards.[1]

My principal was "floored" by this statement. He was totally ignorant that his national association had ever made such an absolute statement regarding the place of moral education in the public school. His reaction, however, was typical — when I brought up the same point during my doctoral studies among a large gathering of administrators, they showed the same shocked surprise exhibited by my high school principal.

The issue, remember, is *who* or *what* is going to determine the *issues* and *direction* of public school education. There are all kinds of individuals or groups that would be very happy to do this for our children and youth.

The implication is simple—somebody is going to tell our children what to do and establish the criteria as to how they are to do it. Criteria established in the past to deal with the problem of violence have not worked.

Violence is a behavior. All behavior is measured by some standard. The athlete's performance is not too difficult to measure; the mile run is measured by a stopwatch; the high jump by a "yardstick;" a basketball player by how many points, rebounds, and steals he makes; a baseball player by his batting average and how many errors he makes. But, when it comes to behavior of the "everyday" variety, we are at a loss to discover a criterion that can act as a standard for workable, desirable behavior.

The Educational Policies Commission of the N.E.A. gives us a hint as to what that standard should be — the development of moral standards. But what moral standards? "Be ye therefore perfect." Is that possible? Hardly, but it does establish a consistent criterion for all individuals who must learn to behave in a productive manner in a rapidly changing society.

What is the basic nature of this perfect behavior? It is love! Broken down into more specific terms, love includes the following behaviors: (1) it is slow to lose patience; (2) it looks for a way of being constructive; (3) it is not possessive; (4) it does not try to impress people nor does it cherish inflated ideas of its own importance; (5) it has good manners; (6) it does not pursue selfish advantage; (7) it is not touchy; (8) it does not keep account of an individual's evil activities — in fact, it is pleased when the truth prevails; (9) it can endure anything; (10) its trust knows no end;

(11) it provides hope for every individual; and most importantly, (12) it can outlast anything, including life as we know it here on earth.

The most practical, everyday expression of the love behaviors I have encountered were expressed in a speech given by Dr. Martin Luther King at the Episcopal Church's General Convention in St. Louis in 1964.

> We must all learn to live together as brothers or we will perish together as fools...Great anthropologists like Ruth Benedict, Margaret Mead...and others, made it clear... they have not found any evidence for the idea of superior or inferior races...
>
> We have been able to stand before our most violent opponents and say we will match your capacity to inflict suffering by our capacity to endure suffering. We will meet your physical force with soul force. Do to us what you will and we will still love you. We cannot in all good conscience obey your unjust laws because non-cooperation with evil is as much a moral obligation as is cooperation with good, and so, throw us in jail and we will still love you. Bomb our homes and threaten our children and, as difficult as it is, we will still love you. Send your hooded perpetrators of violence into our communities at the midnight hours and drag us out on some lonesome, wayside road and beat us and leave us half dead and, as difficult as it is, we will still love you. Send your propaganda agents around the country and make it appear that we are not fit morally, culturally or otherwise for integration, but we will still love you. But, be you assured that we will wear you down by our capacity to suffer and one day we will win our freedom, but we will not win freedom only for ourselves. We will so appeal to your heart and your conscience that we will win you in the process, and our victory will be a double victory...You develop the inner conviction that there are some things so eternally true that they are worth dying for, and if a man does not discover something he will die for, he isn't fit to

live.[2]

Am I fit to live? What do I really believe in? As a teacher, do I believe so strongly in what I am doing that I am willing to give my life for it—this is the ultimate test of love, "that a man lay down his life for his friends."

Are we willing to do this as teachers? I am not suggesting that teachers need to be killed. On the contrary, you can only do this once; but giving your life, daily, for the unloving, and unwanted, misunderstood, handicapped, gifted, etc., is in some way a greater sacrifice.

From 1966 to 1970 I struggled with the other eight members of our Teachers' Negotiating Council in an attempt to improve education for all students in our school district. By 1970, our negotiating platform had a list of 28 items but not once did we ever get past the first two. Number one was teacher salaries and number two, fringe benefits for teachers. We *never* got to those items dealing with student welfare.

It wasn't until about 1968 that the laws of the land finally recognized the fact that students, as students, have rights; and it was not until the early 1970's that the law finally mandated that teachers must bring to the attention of the administration any evidence indicating child abuse. Now in the school year 1979-80, as a professor in a teacher training institution, I am required to teach about discrimination and the public educator. Where have we been as teachers? Why have students rebelled? Do I need the law to tell me how I should be treating the students in my class? When do I say enough? Where do I stand when it comes to the following facts:

1. All individuals who are citizens of the U.S. (including children) have certain rights and these rights are guaranteed by the supreme law of the land, the Constitution.
2. No adult has the right to batter a child, law or no law.
3. No teacher has the right to discriminate against any student for any reason, law or no law.

In the 1960's, students' awareness of their rights found expression in many forms throughout the country. But one Black college professor at Cal State, Los Angeles, described most students as "niggers." They are niggers because at his school the students have separate but equal dining facilities, they are politically disenfranchised; they are expected "to know their place;" even their anger tends to be passive, rather than "active aggression"' But the saddest case, he pointed out, was among both the black slaves and student slaves who so thoroughly took on the values of their masters that their anger is turned inward—these are the kids for whom every low grade is torture, who stammer and stutter when the teacher asks them a question and who go through an emotional crisis at finals time. "If there is a Last Judgment, then parents and teachers who created these wrecks are going to burn in hell."[3]

Students, like black people, this professor pointed out, have immense unused power. They should insist on participating in their own education. They could make academic freedom bilateral. They could teach their teachers to thrive on love and let life come blowing into the classroom. They could tear down another set of walls and let education flow out and flood the streets. They could turn the classroom into where it's at — a feeling of action. . .and believe it or not, they could study eagerly for the best of all possible reasons — their own reasons.

Students, as this college professor pointed out, are about as "powerless" as blacks when dealing with authority figures that control our nation's institutions. Administrators control the public school system, they are responsible for enacting laws and rules which we must have if our schools are going to remain orderly and produce a learning atmosphere that is positive.

But when order becomes the primary goal, then rules, and not students, become the objective. If the student does not fit the mold of the rule he/she is "bounced" out of class. I was under the impression that "rules were made for people, not people made for rules," at least in a democratic society. SUGGESTION: Why not let students have some input regarding the rules in school that are going to directly influence their lives. They are more likely to respect them and also obey them, simply because to do otherwise would be to "cut their own throats." In other words, most students are not going to destroy that which is going to directly benefit them—this is a fact.

How do I know it is a fact? I have seen this principle operate in the high school where I taught. One teacher would have his/her room torn up by vandals. The vandals would skip the room next to it and go tear up the third room. Why did they skip the second room? Why not ask the vandals? The answer might be very revealing.

In the teachers' parking area, specific cars are "hit" more than once by vandals, and yet others go untouched. Why? Ask the vandals. The answers could be most revealing.

A specific English, Social Studies or Physical Education teacher has practically no discipline problems with "trouble-makers," and yet these students, for other teachers, are a constant "headache." Why? Ask the students. The answers could be very revealing.

One teacher says to an angry, frustrated student: "Hit me if it will make you feel better. At least I will understand why you did it." The student replies: "But I could never hit you because I would be hitting someone who cares about me and I could never do that. But I surely would love to go and 'punch out' that teacher who makes me feel so angry."

All of these angry, frustrated, violent students are trying to tell us something, but are we really listening? The psychologist, Arthur Combs, pointed out that the most serious breakdown in communication between a teacher and a student is the failure of the teacher to understand how things *seem to be* to that student.

So, what are these angry students saying to classroom teachers? It *seems* to them that their classroom experiences are anything but "full-filling" for them. They are authoritarian, filled with indoctrination; they are meaningful to the teacher, but students don't get the point; they are centered around the teacher's value system, but they ignore or threaten the student's lifestyle; they do not let the student bring his/her self-concept (lousy as it may be) into the classroom because the teacher perceives that it should be something else.

Teachers can deal directly with this anger and frustration and, thus, reduce the incidents of violence in our public schools. Here are some suggestions for those teachers who truly want to deal with the problem of violence and have the "guts" to do something about it:

Institute love as the guiding principle in your class. In order to do this, consider the following questions:

1. Why do I do something for another person? Do I do it because I want something in return, or do I do it simply

because I want to? Love is unconditional; it has no "strings" attached — all I can do is give it away.
2. If I really love another individual, would I ever ask that person to do anything that he/she did not want to do, or that he/she feels is wrong?
3. How many times am I to forgive? I may not like the act that was committed, but must I still go on loving the individual who committed the act? I may have to reprimand a student, but by my immediate actions I show the student that I still love him/her.

Teachers who can establish this principle of love in their lives will find that their influence will completely dominate the environment of the classroom in a positive way. As a consequence, it is almost impossible to threaten a teacher who is operating under the principle of love. This teacher can say to the class: "Do to me what you will but in the end I will win you over." In other words, students may "do the teacher dirt," but it will stop with the teacher — the teacher has no intention of "getting even." The teacher's intention is to stop the disruptive behavior. Here are some specific suggestions that work — they work especially in times of stress because some of us have tested them out in our classrooms and, as a result, we had very few students get involved in disruptive behavior:

1. "Turn the other cheek" — sometimes the student is right.
2. "Do unto others as you would want them to do unto you" — treat your students as you would like to be treated.
3. "Go the extra mile" — I may be busy or tired, but I still have time for another student.
4. "Practice what you preach" — example is *THE* best teacher.
5. "There but for the grace of God go I" — be patient, especially with the students who are not as fortunate as the teacher.
6. "It is in sharing and caring that life has meaning" — a teacher's life only has meaning in the way that it touches the lives of his/her students.
7. "Give 'til it hurts" — love does not pursue selfish advantage.

8. "The glass is half full, not half empty" — love looks for a way of being constructive.
9. "The way to find your life is to lose it for another" — love is not anxious to impress nor does it cherish inflated ideas of its own importance.
10. "Love has good manners" — good manners are an "outward expression of one's inner feelings."
11. If someone (a student) has "done you dirt," it can stop with you — do not pass it on.
12. "Put-downs" by either student or teacher have no place in a classroom — shame, humiliation, etc. only destroy.
13. "Respect one earns, it cannot be demanded."
14. Happy are those teachers who:
    (1) are *humble-minded* for they realize they do not know everything.
    (2) *know what sorrow means* for they know when their students are hurting and can provide them with comfort and courage.
    (3) *claim nothing* (not even their classroom), for the whole environment of the school will belong to them.
    (4) *hunger and thirst for goodness*, for they will be fully satisfied by the honest efforts of their students.
    (5) *are merciful*, for the students will show the teacher mercy in the time of the teacher's need.
    (6) *are truly caring*, for they will see the good in their students.
    (7) are willing to *practice the way of peace*, for they shall provide hope for the future generations.
    (8) are *truly sincere*, for they will be known as those teachers who are willing to help their students seek the source of *all* truth, beauty, and knowledge.
    (9) are *honest* with their students, for they know that indoctrination does not produce students who are critical thinkers.
    (10) are *willing to make peace*, for they will be known as

those who *practice* peace in their classrooms.
(11) have *suffered for the cause of goodness*, for their efforts will be reflected in the positive behavior of their students.
(12) are the *salt of the earth*, for they help their students develop lasting, useful skills without fanfare.
(13) are the *light of the world*, for their example will guide their students' behavior along the pathway of positive behavior.
(14) *know the law*, for they shall not discriminate against any student at any time.
(15) is not *angry with his brother*, for the teacher who "looks down" on students is "heading for a fall."
(16) *come to terms quickly* with those students who oppose him/her, for the teacher may not get a second chance.
(17) *does not use profane language*, for students will not use profane language in the presence of the teacher.
(18) are *willing to give of themselves* to the students whenever it is asked of them, for students will do the same for such teachers.
(19) *love even the students who mistreat teachers*, for the teacher's reward is found in the loving, not necessarily from the treatment he/she receives from students.
(20) *loves all students*, for what great, noble or good thing has a teacher done if he/she loves only the good and lovable?
(21) can *forgive the faults* of students, for the students can then learn to forgive the faults of the teacher.
(22) learn to *treasure* those things in your students that are of lasting value, for "whatever the teacher's treasure is, there will be his/her heart also!"
(23) learn that they *cannot serve two masters*, for they shall learn that students are more important than money or strikes.
(24) do not *judge or criticize* students, for the "measure

you give will be the measure you get."

(25) *recognize their own faults and limitations*, for in so doing they may be able to help their students do the same.

(26) *treat others exactly as they would like to be treated*, for this is the essence of the practice of love.

Jesus, the teacher, has given us a criterion by which to guide the behavior of any individual who desires to work in a classroom. He points out that all that person has to do is ". . .ask and it will be given to you. Search and you will find;. . .he who asks will always receive; and the one who is searching will always find. . ."

He also points out that the one (teacher) who hears these words and puts them into practice is like a wise man who built his house upon the rock. Down came the rain, up came the flood and beat upon that house — it did not fall because it was built upon a foundation of rock.

But what about the one (teacher) who hears these words and does not put them into action. He is like the foolish man who built his house upon the sand. Down came the rain, up came the flood and beat upon that house — the house collapsed with a great roar.

It is interesting to note that when the historical writer wrote this account of the teaching of Jesus, all who heard Him agreed that His teachings had the "ring of authority."

Does your teaching have the "ring of authority?" It can, but first there is one thing that must be done by the teacher. He/she must develop and *put into practice*, a consistent philosophy of life which becomes the basic foundation for the teacher's educational philosophy. This is extremely important for three reasons: (1) the more consistent the teacher is, the more readily students will know how the teacher is going to act, especially in stress situations; (2) students will also have a better idea of how to deal with the teacher; and (3) consistent teacher behavior will help prevent surprises in the classroom which can create explosive situations.

Explosive situations, all too frequently, lead to violence in a classroom. This does not have to be the case. The teacher should use every reasonable means at his/her disposal to "defuse" a potential violent confrontation with an angry, frustrated student. What means are available to the teacher? The following suggestions, when incorporated in a consistent philosophy of teaching, can help the teacher minimize violent behavior in the classroom:

1. Personal teacher attitudes and/or behaviors:
   (1) Develop and exhibit, in the presence of students, a positive self-concept.
   (2) Feel secure in your own person — if you are, nothing can threaten or intimidate you. It also permits you to let students make mistakes in your class.
   (3) If you are secure, sharing your delegated "power" and "authority" with your students is not very difficult.
   (4) The teacher's willingness to share his/her power and authority, implies that all individuals, including the teacher, are equals — the concept of superior-inferior has no place in the learning process.
   (5) Develop the skill of communicating with students. This not only means dealing with facts, but being sensitive (feelings) to the world in which the student is *now* living.
   (6) Develop the skill to be able to "see how things are" from the student's point of view; can you put yourself in the "student's shoes?"
   (7) I will not let others (students) control my behavior. A student may "hate my guts," but I have no reason to hate him/her. The student has a problem, but I am not going to make his/her problem my problem.
   (8) I will love the student, but I do not like the act (of violence) he has directed at me. I will not add "fuel to a smoldering fire."

   NOTE: REMEMBER, IF YOU HAVE TO USE FORCE TO CONTROL THE BEHAVIOR OF A STUDENT, THE SITUATION IS ALREADY OUT OF CONTROL: YOU MIGHT AS WELL CALL FOR HELP!

2. Class organization:
   (1) "Power" and "authority" in the classroom should be shared by both the teacher and students. The teacher does not give up the authority vested in him/her by the school board, that's asking for trouble. The teacher invites students in the class to share in the exercise of that authority by taking part in a workable democratic process which governs how the class will operate.
   (2) A class organized along the fundamental principles of the democratic process will provide students with *practice* in democratic living.
   (3) A class organized with purpose and meaning will enhance learning experiences for students.
   (4) There should be no "double standard" in the classroom. *All* rules and regulations apply to both teacher and student alike.
   (5) "Invite students in," is an excellent way to prevent violence. If students have direct input regarding the operation of the class, chances are minimal that they will disrupt class activities.
   (6) The rules by which the class operates cannot be arbitrarily changed or altered by the teacher. They can only be changed after consultation and input from students.
   (7) If students know all the rules, then the teacher can be flexible in dealing with all the exceptions that will come up throughout the year. If only the teacher has intuitive access to the rules and expounds on them only at the moment the exception takes place, every exception will soon become a crisis.
   (8) *Trust*, and not power or fear, should be the basis for a teacher's authority. This is accomplished by placing students in a position of trust as well as being honest and sincere in dealing with students.
   (9) *Cheating* — the more competitive the classroom, the greater will be the incidents of cheating.

(10) *Student aides* can help reduce cheating by replacing competition with a "student help relationship."
(11) Do not make an issue over every minor incident — if the teacher continues to do this, students will "tune the teacher out." An issue should only occur when the situation is of such magnitude that drastic action is called for on the part of the teacher. This should be done openly and with the full knowledge of the students.

3. Classroom discipline:
   (1) The teacher must recognize the difference between *discipline* and *learning* as they relate to classroom behavior. Learning involves *active* participation on the part of the student; consequently, the *student controls his/her behavior*. *Discipline* involves external restraint (control) whereby the teacher restricts the behavior of the student. This is not the way to teach students to become responsible for their own behavior.
   (2) An active student is a busy student; thus, he/she does not have time to become a behavior problem.
   (3) Some students enjoy "playing games" if you let them. This kind of psychological fencing can only lead to misunderstanding and mistrust.
   (4) Students who are *challenged* will work, but students who are *threatened* will become a problem. The teacher should remove all forms of threat from the classroom.
   (5) Students who are allowed to make *mistakes* in the classroom will continue to *try* because they know they can learn from their mistakes.
   (6) If a student is led to believe that he/she is a *failure*, he/she will quit trying and probably become a behavior problem.
   (7) The teacher should have *no secrets* in the classroom; the more open the classroom, the less the likelihood of behavior problems.

(8) *Never* back a student into a corner; if a teacher does this, the student will "come out fighting." Create a situation that will let the student find a way out of his/her fix.

4. Students as unique individuals:
   (1) Each individual was created as being unique; therefore, every attempt should be made to protect each student's unique nature.
   (2) Every student is creative in some way. The task of the teacher is to help each student develop his/her creative skills.
   (3) Students, to a large extent, are a product of their environment — let each student bring his/her self-concept and value system into the classroom.
   (4) An intelligent student is one whose behavior is effective, efficient, consistent and produces desirable results.
   (5) One of the major concerns of the teacher should be to help each student develop a positive self-concept —the following factors are part of this development:
      (i) The most important factor is how the student sees himself/herself, not how the teacher sees the student.
      (ii) Success in school has to do with a student's belief in himself/herself; if he/she sees himself/herself positively, the future can be dealt with more effectively.
      (iii) A teacher's *sensitivity* to the world in which the student lives can directly influence the student's behavior.
      (iv) Challenge, do not threaten students; a threat makes a student defensive and angry.
   (6) A student who can develop a positive self-concept is well on his/her way to becoming a *self-actualized* individual. This is a student who is:
      (i) open to new experiences.
      (ii) more likely to be smarter because he/she is

open to all information.
- (iii) more likely to be compassionate and understanding of others.
- (iv) better adjusted.
- (v) more likely to face the truth *accurately* and *realistically*.
- (vi) they learn to *accept* something, but are not *resigned* to it; they are not afraid of the world in which they live because they can cope with it.
- (vii) able to accept himself/herself (acceptance is a learned behavior). A student learns to accept as a consequence of the treatment he/she receives from those who surround him/her.

5. Evaluation of students:
   (1) Students should be evaluated, not rated — rating of students implies acceptance of the superior/inferior concept by the teacher.
   (2) The aim of the teacher's teaching methods should be twofold: (1) to teach students *HOW* to think, not *WHAT* to think; and if you do this then you increase the probability of (2) teaching your students to become responsible for their own behavior. A teacher can accomplish this by doing the following:
   - (i) Presenting materials to your class which represent different points of view.
   - (ii) From these materials, point out to the class the possible courses of action (alternatives).
   - (iii) Help each student *voluntarily* choose the alternative that is best for him/her and *all concerned*.
   - (iv) Let each student *voluntarily* choose the alternative that is best for him/her and *all concerned*.
   - (v) Help each student develop an awareness of the consequences of his/her decision; also, impress

                on the students that the decision is binding.

(vi)   If the student takes action based upon his/her decision and finds the consequences distasteful, help him/her to recycle back through steps (i) through (v) above.

                WARNING: Are you as a teacher secure enough that you can accept a student's decision with which you do not agree, but is the most desirable one for him/her?

    Love is the underlying principle for all the ideas presented in this section of the paper. These ideas can work to reduce violence in the classroom, provided the teacher is willing to incorporate the principle of love in his/her own behavior. The question for all concerned teachers is, am I willing to change *my* behavior so that it becomes a model for my students to copy? If I can become more loving (caring and sensitive) in dealing with my students, it increases the probability that student behavior in my class will become more positive in the future. On the other hand, if I am satisfied with my teaching behaviors and/or methods and am not willing to change, then do I have any right to expect my students to alter their negative behaviors?

CHAPTER FOOTNOTES

    [1]Educational Policies Commission, National Education Association and the American Association of School Administrators. *Moral and Spiritual Values in the Public Schools*, as found in Benjamin S. Weiss, *The Courts and the Schools*, National Educators Fellowship, Inc., pp. 22-23.

    [2]Martin Luther King, Jr., from an address delivered before the Episcopal Society for Cultural and Facial Unity at the Episcopal Church's General Convention in St. Louis, Missouri, 1964.

    [3]Excerpts from a mimeographed paper.

CHAPTER IV

MENTAL HEALTH: ITS ROLE IN NON-VIOLENT BEHAVIOR IN SCHOOLS

The February 2, 1969 issue of the *Christian Science Monitor* made the following observation about the report issued by the National Commission on the Causes and Prevention of Violence:

1. We face a monumental task in getting at the roots of crime in working out ways to curb it.
2. There are three types of violence with which youth are associated: (1) out and out criminality for gain; (2) arson and sniping in the ghettos; (3) violence which often centers around social protest movements.
3. Each of the three types are different, but can have the same end result — all involve wiser social actions; each needs to be better understood.
4. Such understanding is not possible until Americans understand that the mental atmosphere of the entire country needs to be vastly improved.
5. Violence on television and use of firearms are only *symptoms* of what caused the trouble in the first place. What is needed are three things: (1) a deeper sense of law-abiding as found in countries like Switzerland; (2) swifter movement towards solving the country's deep social ills; and (3) some new ways of listening to the complaints of youth and of helping them find corrective, peaceful avenues for existing

violent, disruptive behavior.

The article concluded that the first essential lesson that all Americans need to learn is that violent, disruptive behavior can best be changed through what the Quakers call "gentle persuasion."

David Holstrom, writing in the July 7, 1969 issue of the *Christian Science Monitor*, remarked that "while violence is as historically American as cherry pie," it is not an instinct in man. This same point was emphasized by Dr. F. Werthan in the July 28, 1967 *Time Magazine* essay on "Violence in America." He argues that violence is a learned behavior, not a product of nature, but of society: "The violent man is not the natural but the socially alienated man." The fact is that if violence is not innate, it is a basic component of *human behavior*.

In his book, *The Black Self-Concept*, James A. Banks makes the very pointed statement that:

> Black American has always been angry with White America. Until recently most blacks managed to sublimate their hostilities into channels that would not bring them into confrontation with the dynamite stick or the lynch rope. But an oppressive environment offers a limited number of responses: withdrawal, acquiescence, accommodation, and confrontation.[1]

Banks further points out that the "schools of the nation that watched Watts, Newark, and Detroit burn without perceiving the true message of the flames have been equally imperceptive about the emergence of the new angry black students, the children in revolt in their own corridors." This revolt in the schools, this violence in the schools, according to Banks, is a microcosm of the revolt of black people in American society. And this revolt has changed from a nonviolent direction to one that includes violent conflict.[2]

During the 1960's a number of attempts were made to try and improve the condition of blacks, poor whites, and other minorities in the United States. In spite of such efforts by Dr. Martin Luther King, the Civil Rights Acts, various educational bills, and "the Economic Opportunity Act; the lives of poor people, like the lives of their children in the school, have become more frustrating, more unbearable!"[3]

The sum total of these efforts has left America's minority and poverty-stricken children and youth "still outside of the educational main stream and outside the social mainstream." Compensatory education, according to Banks, was supposed to solve this problem; but it is "ludicrous that white teachers and administration could believe themselves capable of devising special compensatory programs to do the job they were incapable of doing in far more lengthy regular programs."[4]

"However," Banks continued, "failure has not discouraged whites from continuing to dominate and control education of blacks; it has not prevented large cities from continuing to appoint white school superintendents to administer black and Spanish-American majorities."[5]

The 1968 President's Commission on Civil Disorders identified racism as the "corrosive force which is rotting the American fabric."[6] Nowhere, according to Banks, is the effect of white supremacy more pervasive and more debilitating than in American schools. It can be found in many forms: in textbooks, by eliminating the lives and accomplishments of blacks and other minorities; in white teachers who have double standards of expectation, reward, punishment; and it is found in self-hating black teachers who despise their black students.[7]

It is very sad that young people have to threaten and sometimes, through violent action, get the attention of adults within the school as well as the community. The goals of these students "are so amazingly simple, so undeniably just, that rational men must wonder about the wisdom, the morality, even the sanity, of those who would deny their goals..."[8]

What do these children and young people want?[9]

1. They want and need teachers who believe they can learn, who expect them to learn and who teach them: (1) teachers who understand how this perception of the worth and ability of their students directly affects the emotional development and achievement of their students; and (2) teachers who clearly understand that children *want* to learn.
2. They want a curriculum that will release them from psychological captivity. All children must have proof of their own

own worth. "They must be taught to understand and appreciate their cultural heritage by teachers who understand and appreciate that heritage."[10]

Blacks and all minority students not only want a curriculum that is meaningful and inspiring, but they want to be taught by models with whom they can identify and from whom they can derive feelings of worth and pride. According to Banks, any teacher can become this kind of model if he/she is willing to do two things: (1) undergo sensitivity training that will help him/her engage in meaningful self-introspection; and (2) engage in studies about the historical, cultural and educational characteristics of all poor and/or minority groups in America.[11]

James Banks is not alone in his assessment regarding the skills teachers need to work effectively with poor and/or minority students. In 1966 the Cooperative Urban Teacher Education Program was established to better prepare "ghetto-bound" teachers to recognize and accept a culture foreign to their own.[12]

> The value system, mode of living, and socio-economic order encountered in the inner-city are those of another world. Security guards at classroom doors, drop-outs, pupil violence toward teachers, all attest to the obvious lack of communication between the two worlds — of pupil and teacher.[13]

Directors of this program pointed out that most teacher education programs give only cursory attention to matters involving human relations and the mental health of teachers. As a teacher presently involved in the teaching of the core classes of a teacher education program, I can personally support this position. This was pointed out even more dramatically in a survey that appeared in a popular magazine in the late 1960's. The survey indicated that each day three million pupils are exposed to teachers who are so disturbed that they should not be around children. According to the author of the survey, "the school systems must share equally the blame for ignoring the mental health problem." After citing specific instances of mentally unfit teachers, the author indicated that most schools do not have a method of rescuing a "troubled student from the teacher who may be the cause of the problem. Usually the maladjusted teacher continues unchecked for years protected by principals and supervisors whose first loyalty is to the system."[14]

Undoubtedly a majority of teachers are emotionally stable individuals. However, a profession as important to the development and well-being of young individuals and society as teaching is, can ill afford to ignore the problem. The survey continues:

> The schools pay lip service to mental health, teachers take courses in it, and a week is named after it. But the actual mental health of teachers is generally ignored. Anyone who raises the question runs the risk of becoming a pariah to teachers and teachers' organizations.[15]

When the general problems of mental health are considered, evidence indicates that teachers assigned to inner-city, or ghetto schools, confront special problems. And most of these problems stem from the teacher's perception of working conditions in this part of the city. Teachers feel that working conditions in "slum area" schools lack elements vital to their satisfaction and morale, such as small classes, attractive buildings, ample free periods, status recognition and esteem from colleagues.[16]

> In city after city the Negro schools are the most poorly equipped, the oldest, the most crowded. The teachers are ill-trained to work in the slums;...and the buildings are decaying remants of several ages of neglect. Most important, perhaps, is the fact that the teachers — and the system they serve — are conditioned by attitudes as archaic as the buildings in which they work.[17]

Teaching in the "slum area" school has become a most difficult task. Some critics of public education would say the same thing about the schools of suburbia. But no matter where the students come from, the teacher must learn to deal with each child as a child, no matter from what culture he/she comes, no matter what value system he/she brings to school, and no matter how bizarre his/her behavior.

The teacher who is sensitive to the unique character of each student can learn a great deal about the emotions and behaviors of children (as well as his/her own). Thus, the teacher should be better equipped to handle fear, frustration and hostility, and be freer to teach and the student freer to learn.

To avoid explosive educational problems in the classroom, staff members of the Cooperative Urban Teacher Education (CUTE) Program, realized that they needed to help people in their program explore their basic beliefs and reinforce their feelings of self-adequacy.[18] Consequently, the mental health aspect of the CUTE program challenged the participants "to face themselves." The CUTE staff made sure that the participating students were liked, wanted and accepted by the staff. This basically was the format for the mental health program of CUTE.

> People discover their self-concepts from the kinds of experiences they have had with life; not from telling, but from experience. People develop feelings that they are liked, wanted, accepted, and able from having been liked, wanted, accepted, and from having been successful. One learns these things. . .only through the experience of being treated as though it were so. Here is the key to what must be done to produce more adequate people. To produce a positive self, it is necessary to provide experiences that teach individuals they are positive people.[19]

Individuals enter teacher for many reasons. Certainly it is not a selfish occupation. In fact, the psychologist Arthur Combs refers to teaching as the "helping profession." This is possible, according to Combs ". . .in the degree to which the helper (teacher) himself feels basically fulfilled."[20]

Combs, and other contemporary psychologists, have been intrigued by the question of what constitutes an adequate self. Approaching this problem from a perceptual point of view, a highly adequate self seems to be characterized by four general qualities: (1) it sees itself in essentially positive ways; (2) it perceives itself and the world accurately and realistically; (3) it has deep feelings of identification with others; and (4) it is well informed.[21]

In the "Florida Studies in the Helping Professions," and more recent studies on effective teachers, five characteristics were associated with effective helping. In other words, good teachers typically perceive themselves in the following ways: (1) they felt identified with, rather than apart from others; (2) they felt basically adequate rather than inadequate; (3) they felt trustworthy, rather than untrustworthy; (4) they see themselves as wanted rather than unwanted; and (5) they see themselves as worthy rather than unworthy.[22]

"The charcteristics of adequate personalities and the perceptual characteristics of effective professional workers (teachers) are not inherent qualities. *They are learned and what is learned can be taught.*"[23]

Students learn to be loved, wanted, accepted from having been loved, wanted and accepted by "significant other" people. The most "significant other" person in the life of a student is a parent; the second most "significant other" person in a student's life is usually a teacher.

In the classroom, students discover they are wanted or rejected by the reaction of the teacher; consequently, a teacher will have students who exhibit acceptable behaviors if the teacher treats them accordingly. On the other hand, a teacher who behaves in an angry, frustrated, "hateful" manner towards students, will be the recipient of angry, disruptive, and possibly even violent, behavior. The student's anger is the result of the feedback he/she is receiving from the teacher. And if a student receives enough of this kind of feedback in the classroom, it does not take long for that student to develop a pattern of disruptive behavior, thus "tuning out" the teacher and all experiences associated with school. "Why should I respect the school? It doesn't respect me as a person," the student says to himself/ herself. The next step is to "get even" with the school, and this can explode in the form of a violent act toward a teacher, or an act of vandalism toward the school.

Communication between student and teacher does not have to break down. The "lines will remain open" as long as the students respect the teacher; however, a teacher must *earn respect*. It is not automatically granted to an individual simply because he/she holds the authoritative title of teacher. The teacher earns respect by reaching out to the students, and by motivating them to learn. He/she is also an emotionally mature person who knows himself/herself — he/she knows his/her strengths, weaknesses, prejudices, attitudes toward authority, and positive ways of coping with life's problems. "Self-knowledge is a prerequisite to understanding pupils and encouraging them to grow toward self-understanding and self-mastery."[24]

In 1968, Howard James, staff correspondent for the *Christian Science Monitor*, wrote a series of articles dealing with troubled children and youth.[25] One of the articles had the caption: "Schools Don't Have To Make Delinquents." The writer pointed out that:

> public schools too often unwittingly produce delinquents. They do this by inadequate teaching in the lower grades; by letting certain children become classroom goats; by refusing to recognize that there are both 'hand' and 'head' children; by believing they can punish children into learning; and by pushing youngsters with learning problems out of school.[26]

One of the most significant findings reported by James was the fact that youngsters that are given up by the public schools and sent to "forest camps," not only learned to read at these camps, but they liked school.[27]

In his investigation, James found two very important things regarding teachers that are responsible for helping children and youth that have been in trouble: (1) the teachers that were successful in working with this kind of child were *exceptional* teachers; and (2) these exceptional teachers *shunned* traditional teaching methods that were common in the typical public classroom:[28]

> At Public School 148 in New York, a special school for socially maladjusted and emotionally disturbed children, I watched teachers scream and stamp their feet, even hit a child. But the one teacher who was getting through, Miss Flora Boyd, gathered desks into small groups and controlled youngsters by gently touching them. When she graded work she put an arm around the child's shoulder — lightly, naturally.[29]

Wherever James went and found children in trouble learning, the teacher had developed some form of special, warm, intimate relationship with the students. Such a teacher, James pointed out, supplied the student with what sociologists call a "primary group relationship — the warmth and love normally provided by the family and close friends."[30]

In interviews with children and social workers around the country, James found that most delinquents come from homes lacking these qualities. He also found that not all children respond to "intimate, touching relationships." Some seem to respond more readily in situations where the relationship tends to be secondary — where relations are more casual.

James pointed out that schools could do a great deal in helping children who are having academic problems if they would do two things: (1) find out if the child responds better in a primary or secondary group relationship; and (2) find out if there is a "personality barrier" between the teacher and pupil. "If the child needs an intimate (primary) group, or if the teacher is intolerant of his behavior and there is a clash, then changes should be made. This screening would better take place prior to assigning the child to a teacher."[31]

School officials, James found out, complained that they were being handed an impossible task:

> In five or six hours a day they are being asked to tackle problems which the family, church, and community have failed to solve. Educators are being asked to compensate for fractured homes, poverty, slums, stupidity, greed and all the other environmental flaws that contribute to delinquency.[32]

As schools take more and more responsibility for the child, two things appear to be happening, according to James:[33]

1. The breakdown of the family is accelerated. Parents find themselves either left behind or in conflict with what is being taught in the schools.

2. The schools are diverted from their primary goal: teaching children certain basic skills that will enable the youngsters to make their way in the world.

School systems have all kinds of specialists who prod the bright and gifted student on his/her way to college. Yet, in every school system there are many who cannot read, write, or do simple math problems, and find it impossible to find a decent job when they leave school.

Many of these students have specific language disabilities (sometimes called Dyslexia) — it is estimated that about fifteen percent of the public school population has this problem to some degree. This is defined as a disorder in people who:

> ...despite conventional classroom instruction of quality, fail to attain the language skills of reading, writing and spelling commensurate (or equal to) their intellectual abilities to learn. This occurs in the absence of sensory defects, brain damage, cultural deprivation or emotional disturbance as the primary cause.[34]

Children afflicted with this handicap tend to become easily confused, distracted, awkward and forgetful. The letters of our written language he/she does not perceive in the same manner in which they are perceived by children who do not have this problem. These children, however, appear normal and bright in all ways, with one exception. It is this one exception that makes them very confusing to their parents, their teachers and themselves — this exception is the child's ability to keep messages clean, clear, and unscrambled. It means that the message coming to the child's brain through the senses must be properly interpreted in order to be put to use, but in the case of the S.L.D. child, these messages are getting "short circuited."

A traumatic problem arises with these children when the unknowing, or unfeeling, teacher says to the child: "You don't have your work done again. What am I going to do with you?" The student gets frustrated and the teacher gets frustrated. The teacher is constantly "getting on" the student and before long the student either becomes withdrawn or "tunes the teacher out." All the student knows is failure and soon the student's self-concept becomes so negative that it is almost impossible to reach him/her.

My youngest daughter had this problem throughout the first five years of public school. Finally, in the sixth grade, she became part of an experimental program geared to help students who were not too severely handicapped.

At the present time my daughter is in the tenth grade and is experiencing few learning problems. Once in a while a problem does surface when my daughter gets a very traditional teacher who is used to "pushing" students. As a parent I have to do the following things with the teacher: (1) convince the teacher to "back-off" and let my daughter proceed at a slower pace — if she is permitted to do this, she has no problem understanding the material; (2) convince the teacher that my daughter is not dull, slow, stupid, or indifferent; (3) point out to the teacher that his/her traditional teaching methods do not work with her and suggest possible alternative ways of dealing with her; (4) if the teacher persists in treating my daughter in the same manner that he/she has treated all students in the past, she will fail the class; and (5) convince the teacher that failure is not what she needs — she has had an overabundance of this in the past. What she now needs is patient understanding that will help her succeed in the class.

As James researched material for his article on disturbed children, he found that S.L.D. children were not the only ones who were either ignored, misunderstood, or mistreated by school officials. He pointed out that too few schools recognize that there are both "head" and "hand" children.[35]

> A head child is one who deals easily with abstractions...
> or he may be able to memorize from a book. A hand child
> is one who is more practical, often more physically active,
> more concerned with immediate rewards, more caught up
> in material things than vague concepts.
>
> This newspaper's study shows that the hand child is more
> often the one in trouble...Immature, he wants what he
> wants now, not later...Delayed rewards — like a high
> mark on his report card — don't provide him with any
> meaningful payoff.
>
> Such a child usually responds to the attention he gets in
> an intimate primary group, but a large class turns him off.

The same things can be said of the S.L.D. child. The experimental class my daughter was in was small and intimate. Consequently, each child received a great deal of support from other students and the teacher. In a regular classroom such was not the case; in fact, failure was all she had experienced!

Many of the hand and S.L.D. children are imaginative, creative; but all too often these qualities have been channeled into disruptive, violent, or delinquent behavior, rather than into school. Consequently, children and young people who might make important contributions to society are excluded from high school and college and end up in a job that "bores them to death." Instead, youngsters who can sit still and feed back answers like robots have a much better chance of succeeding in school, college and society.[36]

In his newspaper study, James discussed several impressive programs that were designed to help children in trouble.[37]

In Burlington, Vermont, Project Aspire accomplished the following:

1. Convinced two *exceptional* teachers to guide the program.
2. These two teachers exclaimed that the experience made them better teachers.
3. When students in this program were returned to the traditional classroom, they began to fail.
4. To help students make the transition back into the classroom, two *"warm" and sympathetic teachers* were chosen to work with them.
5. Other teachers in the system recognized how *effective the new approach could be.*
6. Burlington High School has changed — *few teachers are worried about their status and rigid professional role.*
7. More *teachers are working with kids*, if not as equals, at least *as real human beings.*

Seattle, Washington Public Schools developed what James called, "another hopeful program" for dependent and delinquent youth. The essence of this program included the following:

1. A *work-study program* where students spent five hours in school per day, and the remainder in vocational work programs.
2. A strong emphasis on *programmed learning with individualized instruction* — a student can go as fast or slow as he/she wants.
3. Emphasis of the program is not only on academic subjects and work skills, but also on *counseling*. "If we can build their self-confidence, give them greater insight into themselves and help them establish goals, then the other comes easily," the program director pointed out.

Albuquerque, New Mexico also established a school for children and youth in trouble, many of them from Mexican-American backgrounds — here are the strengths of their program, according to James:

1. *Four unusual teachers were selected* for the program — each very unique and creative in his/her own way.
2. Both traditional teaching methods and programmed learning were used, but *each teacher employed the technique that he/she found most effective.*

The last school James visited was a high school in Hughson, California. Hughson Union High School is about ten miles from Modesto High School, the school in which I taught for fifteen years. I had the pleasure of visiting Hughson Union High School on a number of occasions. This school was typical of most small, rural high schools found across America — it lacked modern equipment, had poor facilities for the sciences, had a very limited library, and involved a poor program for college-bound students.

The transformation of this school has drawn thousands of educators from all parts of the country to look at the program. What turned this school around?[38]

1. An imaginative superintendent who was determined to educate students better than in traditional schools — he had taught at Modesto High School before going to Hughson.

2. School officials and a Board of Education willing to be re-educated by the innovative Nova School in Fort Lauderdale, Florida.
3. The development of what school officals called "continuous-progress education" — students perform a series of learning tasks at their own speed. When they have successfully completed these tasks, they have earned a grade.
4. Within a given area such as English, the students are given a number of options. There may be 25, but the student is required to complete only eight.
5. These options are written in the form of Learning Activity Packages (LAP). Students work their way through a LAP at their own speed and then take a test on the material when they are ready. If they do not pass the test, they go through some additional activities and take the test again.
6. *Under this system it is almost impossible to fail*, because the student can repeat, immediately, instead of waiting a whole year to take the whole course over.
7. *Teachers* have become *more effective* because they now *work with individuals and small groups.*
8. *Students* with *special problems* have access to a *remedial-reading laboratory.*
9. A student may earn two year's credit in one year or less, depending on his/her ability.
10. *Parental and community involvement* has been tremendous. Adults man labs in the evenings and help teachers as classroom aides during school hours.
11. The school was becoming college-prep-oriented, but several *vocational programs were developed.*

One of the really big dividends of this program has been the reduction of the dropout rate from about twenty-five to zero. Why has this program been so successful? Jerry Carpenter, curriculum coordinator for the school district, points to the following factors as reasons for their success:[39]

1. The system stimulates self-reliance.

2. Students work at their own speed, finding it almost impossible to fail.
3. They are given the option of choosing from a variety of interesting materials.
4. Students know exactly what is expected of them.
5. Each student can develop his/her individual talents.
6. Most importantly, one-to-one help from teachers is available when needed.

Two things, not mentioned in this article, were also responsible for the success of this high school. My visits and conversations with school officials revealed that (1) the entire school board had made a personal commitment in time and money to re-educate themselves and, thus, pave the way for the development of a very non-traditional high school; and (2) that time and money had been spent in re-orienting the entire teaching staff.

None of the successes reported by James in his article could have been possible if the people involved in the education of the children and youth of the community had not committed themselves to a simple truth — that our traditional schools are not getting the job done; consequently, there has to be a better way — each of the aforementioned school districts found a better way!

As mentioned earlier, Hughson Union High School was about ten miles from the high school in which I taught; it would seem that teachers and administrators in our system would have been excited to have, close at hand, a model upon which to draw in order to improve learning conditions in our own schools. In point of fact, only a handful of us took it upon ourselves to become knowledgeable about the Hughson experiment.

Why are a great number of educators literally afraid of programs like those discussed by Howard James in his article?

1. Such programs conflict with the educational philosophy of people in charge of local school districts.
2. Such programs are found extremely threatening by many educators because they bring the teacher and administrator into closer contact with students. They find this personal contact very uncomfortable. Most of them possess the

academic skills to deal with students who have concerns in the various subject matter areas, but they do not have the skills in personal human behavior to cope with the personal problems of students.

Earlier in this chapter, it was mentioned that over three-million children are daily exposed to teachers whose mental health is so bad that it causes problems for students — why don't we get rid of these teachers?

Huntly Collins, a staff correspondent for the *Oregonian*, uncovered some interesting facts relating to this problem.[40] He learned, for instance, that it is most difficult to get rid of a teacher for the following reasons:

1. It is very difficult to find administrators who are qualified to evaluate the performance of a classroom teacher.
2. Administrators do not have the time to do an adequate job of evaluating teachers. In the 15 years I spent in a public classroom I had two visits from one of my administrators that covered an elapsed time of 40 minutes.
3. If an administrator has the skill to do the evaluating, he may be reluctant to use it because of the political problems involved.
4. Rather than creating a "paper trail" of teachers' problems, it is easier to give all teachers a blanket notice of acceptability.
5. The present law in Oregon does not require that an administrator make a *classroom observation of a tenured teacher*.
6. The present law does not require school districts to develop written job descriptions and performance standards on which teachers will be evaluated.

According to Collins, a few districts in Oregon have adopted some new standards for evaluating teachers. These districts have experienced the following favorable results:

1. Teachers have improved their teaching skills.
2. There has been an exodus of incompetent teachers.
3. The new system has helped teachers solve problems when

they have been diagnosed.
4. Supervisors who have undergone training can effectively analyze teacher strengths and weaknesses.

An individual who expects to operate effectively in a public classroom must have command of skills, attitudes, and behaviors in three areas: (1) the individual must be thoroughly grounded in a specific subject matter area; (2) it requires that the individual be just as well informed regarding such areas as theories of learning, theories of personality development, theories of social interaction, theories of educational philosophy, as well as effective contemporary methods of instruction; and (3) a teacher well prepared in areas (1) and (2) will help the students to develop their mental health along positive, productive lines. A teacher with a positive attitude will develop positive students, while a teacher with a negative attitude will produce frustrated, angry students who will "turn the teacher off."

Knowledge of one's subject matter field is not sufficient preparation for an individual who desires to work with children or youth in a contemporary public school. The public classroom is no longer the vehicle for preparing *only* college-bound young people; it is THE vehicle by which *all children and youth of America have the Constitutional right* to an adequate educational experience that prepares them to function effectively in a democratic society. Recognition of this fact is reflected in the present Oregon graduation requirements, which say, in essence, that all teachers are now going to be held accountable for what they do to ALL students who are placed in their charge.

Accountability for all students will no longer permit a teacher to "write-off" students that some teachers ungraciously call "failures," or "stupid," "dumbbells," etc. This means that students with limited ability are capable of learning a few things well, a few things to a limited degree, and some things not at all, no matter what. This does not mean that these students are "failures," it means that we finally recognize that all students have some *personal limitations* and the task of the teacher is to help them to succeed in a public classroom within their limitations. In other words, "Success is the name of the game!"

Hughson Union High School has teachers who know the rules that are involved in the "game of success;" consequently, many of the problems now plaguing other schools have been solved by officials within this school system:

> There is a marked drop in student vandalism, broken windows, kicked-in lockers, and other minor incidents common to most schools. Fights have stopped and students have even established their own dress code.[41]

Teachers and administrators in the districts mentioned by James in his newspaper investigation have all come to the realization that the traditional methods of teaching employed in most public schools in America are not working with the segment of the school population that is a disruptive force in the classroom. If the public schools hope to cope with this problem, the experiments carried on in these schools clearly indicate the following steps need to be taken:

1. Many teachers need to develop skills and attitudes that are more sensitive to the specific, individual needs of *all* students.
2. More teachers need to develop skills that will help them to become more flexible, open-minded and creative in their teaching methods, as well as methods of handling troubled students.
3. Those teachers who find it difficult to deal with non-academic students should not have them assigned to their classes. This only causes frustration and anger on the part of both the student and teacher.
4. The mental health of *all* teachers needs to be given more attention. A teacher who lacks self-confidence is easily threatened, is frightened by new ideas or people with different value systems, should be required to do one of two things: (1) seek some kind of training that can help him/her overcome the problem; or (2) be removed from the teaching profession so he/she can no longer have a negative influence upon our children and youth.

If we are not willing to make these kinds of demands upon the individuals who work in our public schools, are we then ready to pay the price? At the inflated price of things in the economy of the early 1980's, it costs about $2500 to $3000 a year to educate a student — it would cost about $12,000 a year to incarcerate the same individual. Furthermore, an individual educated to be responsible for his/her own behavior will make a greater contribution to society than the person we attempt to rehabilitate behind bars. Which is cheaper? The choice is ours!

CHAPTER FOOTNOTES

[1] James A. Banks, Jean N. Grambs, *Black Self-Concept*, McGraw Hill Book Co., 1972, p. 39.

[2] Ibid., pp. 38-39.

[3] Ibid., p. 43.

[4] Ibid., p. 44.

[5] Ibid.

[6] *U.S. Riot Commission Report, National Advisory Commission Report on Civil Disorder*. Bantam Books, 1968, pp. 2-10.

[7] Banks, *Black Self-Concept*, p. 45.

[8] Ibid.

[9] Ibid., pp 45-47.

[10] Ibid., p. 48.

[11] Ibid., p. 50.

[12] *Now I Have Known Me*. Mental Health Monograph, Cooperative

[29] Ibid.

[30] Ibid.

[31] Ibid., p. 79.

[32] Ibid.

[33] Ibid.

[34] Excerpts from two speeches presented to parents in Shoreline Schools, Sept. and Nov., 1971 by Dorothy M. Revelle, S.L.D. Consultant, Shoreline Public Schools, p. 1.

[35] James, *Children in Trouble*, p. 80.

[36] Ibid.

[37] Ibid., pp. 81-85.

[38] Ibid., p. 84.

[39] Ibid., p. 85.

[40] Huntly Collins, "Teacher Evaluations—Far From Adequate," *The Oregonian*, Portland, OR, Feb. 2, 1980, pp. A10-A11.

[41] James, *Children in Trouble*, p. 85.

CHAPTER V

TEACHERS TEND TO TEACH AS THEY HAVE BEEN TAUGHT
OR
THE PHILOSOPHICAL BASIS OF VIOLENCE

Twenty-five years of adult working life have been spent in the teaching profession. From 1955 until 1970 I taught social studies and coached at the high school level, and since the fall of 1970 I have been a professor in the teacher education program at Linfield College, McMinnville, Oregon. During this period of time I was privileged to do extensive graduate work in the area of educational philosophy. As a result of this work, one thing has become quite evident to me — the vast majority (over 80%) of public schools in America cling to an educational philosophy that is either *regressive* (Perennialism) in nature, or that suggests we maintain the *status quo* (Essentialism).

These philosophies have established assumptions and logical arguments to support their position when dealing with educational problems and issues. Their assumptions and arguments have been the principal motivating force behind the development of policies that have guided and governed most American public schools during the twentieth century. Other philosophies, such as Pragmatism, have provided input in this development process, but their efforts have been minimal.

It is an historical fact that the two philosophies mentioned before have dominated the policies that govern educational trends in most American public school systems. Extant evidence seems to indicate that these policies have not been too successful in dealing with the problem of violence in our public schools. Why?

The answer to this question can be found in some of the elements that support the philosophies of Perennialism and Essentialism — they tend to support the following principles:

1. A belief in an absolute or universal idea.
2. An emphasis on the "essential nature" of things and ideas, not the "particular" or "individual" thing or idea.
3. An emphasis on the human mind (reason) as THE vehicle for attaining considerable understanding of ourselves and the world.
4. A belief that values are pre-determined — we come to know them by objectively evaluating facts and events to which people happen to attach judgments of worth.
5. An emphasis on eternal, intrinsic values.
6. A tendency to set up a hierarchy of values.

An analysis of these principles and beliefs reveals some very significant facts that directly influence the behavior of teachers who adhere to these principles:

1. The teacher's behavior tends to be highly authoritarian in nature. The teacher has acquired "the truth" which never changes. His/her task is to dispense this truth to students.
2. The teacher is THE authority — the students do not question what the teacher presents.
3. The teacher tends to emphasize the "training of the mind" — intellectual excellence is stressed.
4. Subject matter is the major consideration in curriculum matters, not student needs.
5. Indoctrination, via the lecture, tends to be the method of learning employed by the teacher — students are asked to give back to the teacher (the authority) that which he/she asks for.
6. The students play a "passive" role in the learning process. Students learn through the process of formal discipline, memorization, repetition, and preserving our present culture; "learning by doing" plays little, if any, role in the

learning process.
7. All students proceed through the educational process in a "lock-step" method because the curriculum is logically set up to prepare students for that level which is best suited to their nature. Curriculum stresses the "great truths" men have discovered down through the ages.
8. The teacher tends to establish a hierarchy of values — such as honesty, hard work, etc. — the students must measure up to the values established by the teacher because when the student is properly trained (the teacher determines this) he/she will choose the *proper value at the highest level*.
9. The teacher will employ *any* method of instruction that helps the student reach the predetermined goals established by the teacher — consequently, ENDS are the major consideration, while MEANS are almost completely ignored.
10. The *aim* of education for the teacher is intellectual excellence; consequently, the stress is placed on teaching students WHAT (subject matter) to think, not HOW (problem-solving) to think.

There are some very interesting "spin-offs" that occur in classrooms that are conducted by teachers who hold to this philosophy:

1. Classrooms become highly competitive — competition arises when there is not enough of the valued commodity (high grades) for all concerned (students).
2. *Rivalry* (competition at a very personal level) develops in a highly competitive classroom. In such an atmosphere, competition tends to become more keen and hostile, thus giving rise to antagonistic competition or social conflict.
3. *Cheating* — the more competitive the classroom, the higher will be the incidents of cheating, simply because reaching the goal (end) is more important than how (means) the student got there.
4. *Tracking* of students by means of standardized testing is of major importance in order to identify the slow, average and

talented student.[1]
5. *Bored* students, due to subject matter that has little to do with their personal needs, interests, and aspirations.
6. Students learn how to *"regurgitate"* knowledge, but have little practice in problem-solving.
7. Students who make mistakes (get low test scores) or *challenge* ideas presented by the teacher are penalized (low grades) for their efforts.
8. Any student behavior not approved by the teacher is considered deviant and, therefore, it will be punished.
9. *Flexibility* is not permitted; nor are individual student differences given much consideration — *all* students must abide by all rules, no matter what the circumstances.
10. *Conformity* becomes the "watchword" in the learning process, not creativity.
11. *Passive student behavior* is rewarded — this means that the room is quiet; therefore, the teacher must be "doing a good job," even though the students might be bored stiff.
12. *Discipline* is a matter of teacher control — little consideration is given to having the students take an *active* role in "becoming responsible for their own behavior."
13. *Verbal intimidation* (threat), by the teacher, becomes a common method of "keeping students in line."

Perennialistic and Essentialistic thinking educators have dominated the public school scene in America for the past one hundred years. Listed above are examples of some of their educational beliefs, values, attitudes and behaviors. If these are a reflection of the major elements that have been in control of American public schools, then one would have to conclude that they have been a miserable failure in trying to cope with the problem of violence in the public schools.

Common sense would seem to dictate that, "what did not work in the past, probably will not work in the future." But, according to some educational research projects in the 1950's and 1960's, one finds that a public school teacher "tends to teach and think as he/she has been taught."[2] Apparently, the majority of young people coming out of our teacher-training institutions are going into the public classroom with an educational philosophy founded on the principles of Perennialism and/or Essentialism. No wonder the majority of teachers who appeared on the October 21, 1979 "Town Hall" TV program aired from Portland, Oregon, admitted that they had developed little, if any, skill in dealing with violence in their classrooms.[3]

A Black high school senior who appeared on this program made one of the most significant observations during the show. The adult participants on the show were discussing reasons why students disrupt classrooms, attack teachers, and vandalize teachers' property. Most of the responses indicated frustration and little understanding of the problem. The Black, young lady responded to the adult bewilderment by pointing out that *verbal abuse* directed at students by teachers was one of the major causes of the problem. The abused student, she emphasized, does not necessarily react immediately, but will, in most cases, walk out of the room full of resentment because of what the teacher has done to him/her. His/her resentment, she continued, might show up in a number of different ways, such as vandalizing the teacher's car, the school, or school property, or "lie in wait" and "get even" with the teacher at a later time.

Not one adult in the studio audience reacted to the young lady's comments. I was flabbergasted! I thought at least one of the teachers would feel threatened by her comments and, at least, become "defensive," — it did not happen; furthermore, no one came to the defense of her point of view — NOTHING! The discussion went on as if this very perceptive high school senior had not uttered a word.

I remember a phrase I picked up as a child from my church school teacher: "A soft answer turneth away wrath." In a classroom a teacher does have absolute authority, but the *exercise* of that power is the key to student behavior. Abuse of this power will ultimately lead to negative student behavior because "power tends to corrupt, and absolute power tends to corrupt, absolutely." This can be prevented if the teacher is willing to *share* his/her power with the students; however, a teacher whose philosophical orientation tends to be authoritarian in nature would find it difficult to permit such sharing — sharing implies methods of dealing with students which are flexible, flexible to the point of possibly letting students select from competing alternatives which might be contrary to the position held by the teacher. The authoritarian teacher, by definition, would not condone such practice in a classroom. He/she would, nevertheless, act in a very consistent manner but in a manner consistent with a belief that he/she alone (with the approval of the administration) has the absolute right to determine the standards of conduct for the students in his/her classroom. Consequently, here are some typical attitudes and/or behaviors such a teacher might exhibit in his/her classroom:

1. The *superior/inferior attitude* will prevail because the teacher is the absolute authority; the role of the student is to accept the "truths" offered by the authority figure (the teacher).
2. *Subject matter* will be the major focus of the learning process, not student needs and aspirations.
3. Maintaining the *status quo of the class*, and not individual differences of students, will be emphasized by the teacher.
4. *Student discipline* will be one of the major problems confronting the teacher — he/she would tend to approach it in the following manner:

    (1) The teacher would be responsible for the conduct of students' behavior.
    (2) Student movement (psychological, intellectual, etc.) would be minimal.
    (3) A common practice, "to keep students in line," would be the use of *verbal threats*.
    (4) Little, if any, flexibility would be permitted when rules are violated.
    (5) Punishment, not reinforcement, would be stressed — students who violate rules would be punished (rather than counseled) by doing extra work, staying after school, drop in grades, or "kicked out of school."
    (6) There would be a constant "battle of wits" or "game playing" going on between teachers and students — teachers often refer to "drawing the battle-lines" between them (students) and us (teachers); consequently, it becomes a "battle for survival" in the classroom.[4]

(7) *Respect* the teacher *demands*, but the students say to the teacher, "You will have to *earn* it."

(8) *Trust* is a matter of obeying the rules set down by the teacher, not placing students in situations where they have to "answer for their own behavior."

5. Teachers would tend to use the following methods of instruction in their classes:

(1) *Lecture*, in order to dispense information that students are usually asked to give back to the teacher in some form of objective test; problem-solving and/or group work would be "out!"

(2) Teachers would tend to *stereotype* students in terms of slow, average, bright.

(3) *Grades* would be stressed — they would be used in terms of reward or punishment rather than a measure of student progress.[5]

(4) *Student progress* would be measured in terms of *predetermined* teacher criteria and/or goals, not in terms of "where the student is now and how far he/she was able to get" during the class.

(5) Classroom materials, such as textbooks, workbooks, units, etc., are usually selected on the basis of the teacher's background, training and educational orientation, not on the basis of students' cultural, social, academic or vocational needs.

(6) Students are *motivated*, in general, out of *fear* of the teacher; not out of *respect* for the teacher, or subject matter being discussed — "you had better do what the teacher tells you, or else!"

6. *Intelligence* is a fixed attribute that can be accurately measured via the use of standardized tests.[6]

7. There would be a tendency to *acculturate*[7] racial and/or minority students rather than treating them as members of a "pluralistic society."[8]

An honest question might be asked at this point: am I being fair, or just, in my assessment of teachers who advocate the educational philosophies discussed on the previous pages? I would like to point out two things: (1) I am aware of the dangers inherent in the process of "generalizing;" and (2) I know there are some excellent public school teachers who are so oriented but are having a positive influence upon the lives of their students; however, they are "few and far between."

There is an old saying; "If the shoe fits, wear it;" but if the shoe pinches, whose fault is it! You put the shoe on, and you can take it off. *Only you can change it!* So, let's be honest! If you are having trouble with disruptive behavior in your classroom, whose fault is it? Aren't you in charge of the class? Isn't the teacher authorized by the school board to be responsible for the atmosphere, or learning environment, that is established in a given classroom? Is it the school board? How about the principal? Maybe it's the community or the parents? If not, then maybe we can "put the blame" on the students. BUNK! Any teacher who has spent extended time in a classroom knows THE TEACHER is responsible for the activities that take place within his/her classroom. If a teacher says this is not true, then I suggest he/she is not being honest, and if he/she cannot be honest with himself/herself, then how can he/she be honest with his/her students? Students need a model they can trust and respect; someone who can be a confidant or a friend, particularly when the student is caught in a "sticky situation." He/she does not need an adult, authority-figure "getting on his case" by pontificating upon his/her "naughty behavior." What he/she needs is HELP, not advice, or "value judgments" thrown at him/her which are irrelevant to his/her immediate emotional condition. He/she may hear the "bellowing" teacher, but it is just "going in one ear and out the other." Why? Simply because nobody likes to be treated in such a fashion, and "bellowing" at a student will only make him/her more defensive and angry.

There are some very specific factors operating in classrooms dominated by teachers who approach their teaching tasks from an authoritarian point of view. The following factors exist whether we like it or not; to ignore them is not going to make them "go away:"

1. *Fear* — the teacher makes sure the students "know who is boss."

2. *Threat* — a student is threatened by anything in a classroom that he/she cannot handle.
3. *Negative teacher attitudes* — "put downs" and humiliation are common forms of teacher behaviors that he/she uses to control students.
4. *Bored students* — the information does not come across as being valid and/or relevant to students.
5. *Power struggle* — "it's them or us."

A very wise man asked "God grant me the serenity to accept the things I cannot change; courage to change the things I can; and the wisdom to know the difference." In our attempts to deal constructively with violence in the classroom, it might help if we applied this wisdom to the five factors listed above. Any teacher who has the courage to change what he/she can, and accept what he/she cannot change, will at least make an attempt to eliminate these factors from his/her classroom.

FEAR — how can it be eliminated from the classroom; here are some suggestions:

1. The teacher should deal with his/her own feelings and emotions so when he/she steps into a classroom, he/she is secure in himself/herself.
2. Fear produces anger, hate, frustration, etc.; the teacher should avoid the use of words and/or actions that arouse these negative feelings in himself/herself and his/her students.
3. Some teachers tend to confuse the two terms: *fear* and *respect*. How many times have I heard, "The students will respect me, or else." Or else what — with an attitude like that, I doubt if the students will develop much respect for that teacher.
4. Respect one earns! As students and teacher develop a feeling of mutual respect, fear diminishes in the classroom. This happens when the teacher treats students with dignity and worth.
5. The teacher should not *dominate* students; he/she should

respect their feelings and opinions.
6. *Trust* is developed by eliminating the "double standard" — "what is good for the teacher is good for the students."

THREAT — the elimination of threat should be a primary consideration if the teacher hopes to have positive learning experiences take place in his/her class. Consider the following alternatives when dealing with this problem:

1. Remember, a student becomes threatened when he/she is involved in a situation he/she cannot deal with — help him/her to "find a way out."
2. *Be sensitive* to anything that might threaten a student in your class. Example: a student who cannot read will be threatened by a reading assignment. A student with poor eyesight might be threatened by an assignment written on the blackboard.
3. The *perceptions* of a threatened student are narrowed, thus eliminating possible alternative ways for him/her to deal with his/her problem.
4. A threatened student is forced on the defensive, thus making it next to impossible for the student to become involved in a new learning experience.
5. Threatened students usually "fail." "Success is the name of the game." A teacher removes threat by *challenging* students. A student is challenged when he/she faces a new experience that does not overwhelm him/her, but in an attempt to cope with the situation he/she will be permitted to make mistakes if it will help him/her in the end, to succeed.
6. Eliminate shame, humiliation, or failure experiences which make the student feel like a "no account."
7. Unique, open, flexible, and creative approaches to learning, applied by the teacher, can help to remove threat.
8. Let students make *mistakes* — a student who is afraid of making a mistake *will not try*!
9. Find more ways of becoming more sensitive to the world in

which students live — become more sentitive to how they *feel, think,* and *perceive.*

NEGATIVE TEACHER ATTITUDES — do you want to be more positive in dealing with your students? "Try these on for size:"

1. Learn to *communicate* with students. Teachers can do this by understanding how things *seem* to students they are working with. A teacher who fails to recognize this fact is making a very serious mistake in dealing with students — it is "not a question of how things are, but how they seem to be." Example: try explaining to a "love-sick" teenage girl that all the facts indicate she should not marry her mature lover who is in his forties.
2. Learn the skill of *acceptance* — help students to accept themselves as they are, limitations as well as strengths. Students learn to accept as a **consequence** of the treatment they receive from those who surround them — make them feel *needed* and *wanted*. If a teacher can do this, then students learn they do not have to be resigned to what they are, but they learn that they can "become" more than what they are.
3. Eliminate "put downs," use of phrases like "shut up," "stupid idiot," or innuendoes that degrade.

BORED STUDENTS — there are three kinds of "drop outs" that invade our public schools: (1) the student who never shows up (for whatever reason); (2) the student who shows up periodically; and (3) the student who shows up every day and occupies a seat in class, but whose mind is elsewhere. The first two categories of students are not too difficult to identify; the third, however, is not only difficult to identify, but most school officials fail to recognize students who fit into this category as drop-outs — the body is present, but the mind is absent and "never the twain shall meet." Consequently, they become "flunk outs," "push outs" or just plain failures.

These students are just plain bored! Why? The reasons are simple — the teacher:

1. does not enjoy teaching, and the students can sense it.
2. is a lousy salesman — his/her enthusiasm "got left at home," so students go to sleep.
3. knows his/her subject, but does not know how to "get it across" to students.
4. feels he/she is superior to students and students resent his/her attitude.
5. uses the "same old method" (lecture) to present material to his/her class.
6. does not involve students in the learning process.
7. uses the same old materials (and tests) year after year.
8. is more interested in activities outside of school; consequently, he/she does not get involved with students in activities outside of his/her class.
9. does not really care about students, so why should the students care about what goes on in class.
10. is not able to make his/her subject matter relevant to his/her students' needs, interests, and aspirations.

POWER STRUGGLE — in the late 1960's and early 1970's, the "power struggle" between students and teachers (including administrators) came to a boil. The resulting violence and destruction is now a fact of history. During this period of turmoil, I was teaching in a racially-mixed California high school. Those were exciting days — exciting because things were happening in the public schools. For the first time in the history of public secondary education, students began questioning some of the rules and regulations that made little sense to them. Dress codes, pregnant girls attending school, student government that had little "teeth in it," equality of opportunity for all students, were a few of the issues that surfaced within our public schools.

What were some of the issues that caused these problems to explode on the educational scene in the 1960's and 1970's?

1. Specific student and teacher rights and responsibilities were identified and upheld by the courts.
2. Specific groups such as Blacks, Chicanos, American Indians, Orientals, the handicapped, were being denied equal access

to educational opportunities in our public schools; they began asking for the same educational privileges enjoyed by the majority white population.
3. The emergence of specific cultural groups who wished to maintain their own cultural identity — this raised questions concerning the omission of certain specific cultural materials within existing school curricula.
4. The emergence of the concept, "Democracy Is A Dangerous Doctrine."

    a. It rejects *indoctrination* as a valid learning process.
    b. It rejects the *authoritarian* teacher as THE only source of information and/or truth.
    c. It presents alternative points of view.
    d. It encourages students to probe, question, seek out all information.
    e. It encourages students to question established institutions, procedures, rules, mores, etc.
    f. It transfers learning from the restrictive confines of the classroom to the "world at large."
    g. It teaches students *how* to think.
    h. It teaches students to become responsible for their own behavior.

A positive reaction to this latter issue was the development of curriculum materials which focused on the problem of "values clarification." The work of such writers as Lawrence Kohlberg, James Shaver, William Strong, Louis Raths, Merrill Harmin, Sidney Simon, Fred Newman, Donald Oliver, Virginia Hash, James Banks, and Jack Frankel stressed the need for students to develop the skills to identify, analyze, and assess alternative policies and procedures that can help make them make intelligent choices.[9] Many teachers, including myself, hailed the efforts of these educators as a real breakthrough in combatting the stranglehold the authoritarian curriculum has maintained on the American system of public education. It looked like the public schools of the 1970's were finally going to "take unto themselves" curriculum materials that would help our children and youth develop the critical thinking skills that are so necessary if an enlightened democracy is to work.[10]

The excitement of this effort has been short-lived. Three incidents took place in Oregon between the fall of 1978 and January, 1980 which illustrate the fate of the values clarification movement.

1. At the Fall, 1978 State Conference of Social Studies teachers, Jack Frankel and Walter Hus[11] were the keynote speakers. Mr. Frankel presented the rationale for the values clarification curriculum, while Walter Hus defended the "going back to basics" curriculum expounded by Max Rafferty in California during the 1960's. The general reaction of the social studies teachers surprised me. They were very cordial during Mr. Frankel's presentation; however, Mr. Hus' presentation evoked an enthusiastic reaction from the audience.

2. A number of school districts in Oregon have either dropped completely from their courses of study, values clarification materials, or altered them to the point of rendering them ineffective.

3. In January, 1980, the Oregon State Board of Education announced that in the fall of 1980, all high school students would be required to take one full year of American history. Traditionalists feel that such a requirement will help students become better citizens.[12] A similar attitude in California in the 1960's was responsible for all students being required, by law, to repeat the pledge of allegiance before the start of school each day. To assume that such requirements will guarantee the development of young minds capable of running a democratic nation is pure nonsense. Common sense dictates better results are achieved by taking part in an activity, not by reading about it.

I spent two years of extensive research throughout the entire State of California gathering information for my dissertation. One of the things I learned was the overwhelming fact that students identified American History as the subject they "hated" most. The problem was not the subject matter itself, but the way it was being taught. In general, it was taught as a course full of factual information that was unrelated to the lives of the students.

I found, from my own experience of teaching American History, that it does not have to be taught that way. I helped to develop, along with one of my colleagues, what we called the "reflective-confrontation" method of teaching American History. This method of instruction related the history of the past to events that were taking place in the contemporary lives of students — the students "ate it up."

Dr. Max Rafferty epitomizes the Perennialist philosophy of education that is critical of any standard or doctrine that does not support his position. Dr. Rafferty's abysmal ignorance regarding some of the principles inherent in John Dewey's Pragmatic educational philosophy[13] is reflected in the following passage from his book, *Suffer Little Children*:[14]

The children were not the only sufferers. The nihilistic leveling that was so much a part of the Progressive credo inflected the very essence of Education itself, in the person of the classroom teacher. Since subject matter was ephemeral, unreal, why should the teacher know anything. Intellectualism became suspect. Insistence upon standards declined as the teacher's own standards dwindled...

Further on in his volume, he declares that the "only one great problem in American Education...is the tragedy of declining standards." The standards, according to Rafferty are intellectual:

Our teachers...today know more about mental hygiene than those who went before, but less about the English language. They are far more at ease in the field of handicrafts, but far less so in a discussion of historical figures or events. They have more instructional techniques at their disposal than did their forebears, but fewer resources in the realms of literature and art.

...I have heard it argued that deterioration in the field of general culture...is unimportant. "After all, the teacher can turn the child into an integrated member of a democratic society," it is said, "that is the significant thing." The child's ability to make optimum adjustments, to solve meaningful problems, and to work creatively with his hands are the major goals of modern teaching. Whatever subject matter is selected to implement these objectives should always be considered the means to an end, never as a goal in itself.[15]

Dr. Rafferty blames the teacher education institution for the downgrading of the teaching profession:

...they have stressed the *how* rather than the *what*. They have literally welcomed all comers into the profession without stopping to examine intelligence,[16] literacy, or erudition until it can be seriously said that anyone above the moron level who possesses...time, money, and perseverance can get a master's degree in education from any institution...that offers it.[17]

While Max Rafferty was making his way through the trials of his preparation for the teaching profession, he pointedly remarked that one of his professors lied to him because he used to say: "The content of the subject taught is of minimal importance. What is significant are the attitudes and values which rise out of the interrelationship of the teacher and the pupil."

"They actually believed this stuff," Rafferty exclaimed. Not only that but, according to Rafferty, "teaching children self-actualization was a waste of our country's precious resources of brains and talent."

Sputnik, Rafferty pointed out, put an end to all this. No longer could curriculum consultants say that woodworking was as important as physics. Consequently, Rafferty believed that America's survival depended upon the students of chemistry and calculus and languages rather than upon the worthy patrons of the working crafts that sustain our American way of life.[18]

Using Dr. Rafferty's own words, "and he actually believes this stuff!" What a tragedy! He, and others who support such "bull" need to climb down out of their "ivory towers" and "rub shoulders with the children of the ghetto and the rest of us "common folk" from "middle America." The elitist attitude expressed by Rafferty is a "slap in the face" to the principles that support our democratic way of life. He, and most of the supporters of the "Back to Basics" movement, would have us believe that they have the answers to our educational woes. The ignorance of those who advocate such a move is not only shameful, it is frightening. They fail to consider the following factors:

1. Historically, the youth population that attended our public high schools has increased, since World War II, from about sixty percent to close to ninety-five percent in 1980.
2. Part of the motivation for creating public high schools in America was to get the youth of our nation out of the coal mines and "sweat shops" of industry; they were not created to produce an elite class of young "brain-trusts."
3. The number of young people graduating from high school between 1945 and 1980 has increased from about thirty-five to sixty-five percent.
4. The basic curriculum of most high schools during this same period of time has remained college preparatory in nature; yet less than fifty percent of our present high school graduates finish college. This has given rise in recent years to a tremendous growth in vocational and career education as well as work experience programs. The intent of such programs at the high school level is to help the large non-college-bound school population develop the skills that will help them "make it" in our society.
5. Historically, handicapped and mentally retarded children have been excluded from the mainstream of American public education. Title VI, Title IX, and Public Law 94-142 have put an end to this discriminatory practice.
6. Historically, the authoritarian dogma that permeated the policies established by administrators, has tended to keep the general public out of the public schools, made it diffi-

cult to pass bond issues, caused teachers to go out on strike, and alienated students. The courts, in the late 1960's and 1970's, established the principle that teachers, students, and parents have rights under the law that must now be protected by administrative codes, rules and regulations.

If one considers these factors — as well as others not mentioned — it becomes obvious that public school of today is not the public school of thirty years ago, and the same is true of the school population. The present school generation has to try and cope with such problems as nuclear contamination, genetic engineering, cybernetics, and the computer age, that were unknown to the schools of the 1940's. If the present youth generation hopes to cope with the problems created by these scientific innovations, it *must* master the "basics" of learning — reading, writing, and computing. Without the "basics" this generation would be void of even the most primitive skills that are essential for survival in our growing technological society, let alone the more sophisticated skills required to meet the demands of a complex social order.

In other words, educators do not need to "go back to the basics," the "basics" are already being taught in our public schools. The problem is not one of going back, but one of *doing* a more adequate job of teaching the basic skills of reading, writing, and computing. *All* teachers, in every subject area, at all grade levels of public education, should be working on these skills. If they are not, then they are violating, not only the terms of their teaching contracts, but the basic principles of good teaching. How in heaven's name is a high school student going to understand the Bill of Rights if he/she cannot read? How is he/she going to learn the skills necessary to make out a grocery list, or complete an income tax form if he/she cannot read, write and compute? We don't need to go back to anything. What we need is to employ dedicated teachers who are willing to accept the limitations of students which are brought into the classroom and help them improve their meager skills. Such dedication requires the development of a highly self-actualized teacher who is sensitive to, not only the academic needs of students, but also their personal, social, emotional and spiritual needs. Max Rafferty would say, "Hogwash, we don't need self-actualized teachers; what we need are intellectual giants who are versed in the classics."

I am reminded of a story that hit the front page of the newspapers of California in the late 1950's. A young woman who was pregnant contracted paralytic polio. In order to help her give birth to her baby, a highly trained, special doctor was assigned to her case. A few days later the headline read: "Doctor Rapes Patient." Here was a brilliant man who possessed skills above and beyond those of most of his colleagues. But what good were his intellectual capabilities to this young woman he was supposed to aid in a time of stress?

There is one other aspect of the Max Rafferty philosophy that I find disturbing. The authoritarian nature of this philosophy does not permit the inclusion of possible alternative choices when dealing with subject matter. I find this disturbing because of the situation our nation is faced with at the start of the 1980's. Iran is holding some of our people hostage, and Russia has invaded Afghanistan. There are many in our country who say that the only choice left open to us in dealing with such problems is the use of force. The authoritarian philosophy of Rafferty would tend to support such a position.

This philosophy applied to a classroom situation could have very devastating results. In essence, it would say: "The best way to meet force is with force." If a student disrupts a classroom with some form of violent behavior, he/she will be treated in a similar fashion. In other words, there are no alternative options open to the student or teacher. There is only one way to deal with a violent student in a classroom, and that is to retaliate with some form of force. No wonder violence tends to be perpetuated in our public schools.

Max Rafferty did his best to impregnate the California State System of Public Education with his philosophy of education. Prior to his tenure as State Superintendent of Public Instruction, from 1962 to 1968, the public schools of California ranked as having one of the best systems of public education among all of the fifty states. By 1968 this ranking had fallen to a point that it could not be classified among the top twenty-five.

During this same period of time I was teaching in a high school in Modesto, California. A colleague of mine, who taught in the English Department, was a staunch support of Dr. Rafferty's teaching philosophy. Quoting from Dr. Rafferty's own words, this English teacher was characterized as one of the "intellectual elite" of our staff, who was extremely "erudite" in the classics. I was checking in one morning when this teacher, who was standing at my elbow, suddenly turned to me and said: "I may have to teach these stupid kids, but don't ask me to love the bastards!" He was fired at the end of the year and Dr. Rafferty was finally turned out of office in the election of 1968 after he had left the State System of Public Education in California in chaos.

I had the opportunity to listen to Dr. Rafferty on several occasions. He was a master of the spoken word. His "silver-tongued" oratory was extremely persuasive. He had the ability to convince most of his audience that, under his leadership, he could lead the public schools of California out from under the yoke of Dewey Progressivism and into the saving sunlight of Perennialistic "regressivism," which is patterned after the elitist educational system of the classical Greek era.

After listening to one of his presentations, I said to a group of my colleagues who were also in attendance: "Did you really hear what he had to say?"

"Why sure, Tom, wasn't he wonderful?"

"You have got to be kidding! You heard his words, but you were not *listening* with a critical mind. His eloquent use of the English language," I pointed out, "is a 'smoke screen' to hide the principles he espouses."

What are some of these principles? I think it is important for every public school teacher to know what they are. Why? Simply because the present trend in education to "go back to the basics" is another way of saying what we need to improve contemporary American public schools is a return to what Dr. Rafferty supports. Here is what he supports. Ask yourself, is this what we need to help solve the problems of disruptive behavior that is plaguing our schools?

1. A system of elite education that would put most of its money and energy into programs for the highly gifted students — little would be left for the majority of the school population.
2. The aim of education would be the acquiring of knowledge, while problem-solving would be ignored.
3. Discipline, control of student behavior by the teacher would be stressed; while the process of helping students become responsible for their own behavior would be ignored.

4. The stress would be placed on college preparatory, academic subjects, to the exclusion of vocational, career education and work experience programs.
5. The high schools would no longer be "comprehensive" in nature. Their function would not be to help *all* students develop the skills they would need to function in their community; but they would become strictly college preparatory institutions or "brain factories."
6. There would be little, if any, room in the curriculum for helping students become self-actualized individuals. Values such as caring and love would give way to strictly academic pursuits.
7. Students would be indoctrinated to accept the wisdom of the teacher without question.
8. One of the most devastating elements of this philosophy is contrary to the basic principles of our democratic way of life — here are some examples:
    a. Value judgments of teachers could literally "make or break" students — this student is bright, but this student is dull.
    b. Students would be educated for their "proper role" in society — according to who?
    c. Students who are properly trained will choose the proper value at the highest level — according to who?
    d. Handicapped or slow students would be almost completely ignored under this system of education.
9. This philosophy assumes that those who qualify as the intellectual elite are, therefore, THE individuals who are qualified to lead — this assumption would be most difficult to defend.

This assumption, and others inherent in the philosophy described above, are a mockery to the eighty-five percent of Americans who do not fit into the category of the intellectual elite. The public schools of America belong to *all* who inhabit our shores, and each individual, regardless of his/her ability has, by law, the right to a free, quality education in a public school. Any philosophy of education, or individual who supports such a philosophy, is condoning a practice of discrimination that has been outlawed by recent legal statutes. The federal law provides in 42 U.S.C., Section 1983 that:

> Every person who. . .subjects or causes to be subjected any citizen of the United States. . .to the deprivation of any rights, privileges, or immunities secured by the Constitution and laws shall be liable to the party injured in an action. . .or other proper proceeding for redress.[19]

A free public education is a right guaranteed to every citizen. Each state has the responsibility for carrying out that right for those children and youth who reside in the state:

> . . .An employee of a school may be liable for violation of rights guaranteed to teachers, staff or students (if) . . .
>
> 1. The employee knows the law and violates it on purpose.
> 2. The employee violated the law without actually knowing it, but should have reasonably known that the law existed and that the action the employee took violated the law.[20]

Max Rafferty, and some educators who advocate the "back to basics" movement, ignore one fundamental fact of American public education. At least eighty percent (it could be much higher) of our contemporary public schools adhere to some of the principles that are part of Rafferty's Perennialistic philosophy of education, and not the Pragmatic principles established by John Dewey. In other words, what these critics need to do is analyze the principles of their own educational philosophy. They are the principles which are presently guiding the destiny of most American public schools. How can they blame John Dewey, or any innovative educator, who does not claim allegiance to their following, for the ills that beset our public schools? If violence (disruptive student behavior) is a problem in our schools, then the philosophy that spawns that behavior needs to critically examine its basic assumptions. These assumptions support the rationale for the dogmatic methods of instruction employed by the majority of people now teaching in our public schools. Apparently these methods of instruction are frustrating and unfulfilling to many high school students. Here are some graphic examples taken from my personal involvement in public education during the 1960's and 1970's.

Back in 1974 I was asked to speak at a state teachers' convention in Stockton, California. After the convention I drove to Modesto, California where I had taught high school for fifteen years. I contacted the blind teacher I had team taught with and asked if I could visit some of his classes. Manuel's reply was most interesting:

"Tom, we would enjoy having you visit our old classes, but don't be surprised if half the students don't bother to show up."

"I don't understand, Manuel, we never had trouble getting the students to come to class when we worked together."

"Things were different then, Tom. We did our thing and developed materials that were relevant to the needs of our students, Now, it's back to the same old traditional materials that not only bore the students, but I'm just as bored."

In the late 1960's Manuel and I team taught American History. This approach permitted us a great deal of flexibility. The results of this approach are reflected in the following comments made by one of the most brilliant students that ever came through our classes.

Zandra Illick, in her paper, "I Don't Want To Be Ignored," expressed the frustration that many exceptional students encountered during their high school days:

> I have no ambition to be ignorant in any aspect, yet I reserve the right to an absence of knowledge in a given area. I have found that, at times, this right is not always in my hands. The omnipotent rule of the present school administration and curriculum system is a planned obstacle course, offering me pleasures and pain, according to my limping aptitudes and intelligence quotient. The courses open to my discretion, and those shoveled onto my doorstep, are in accordance with the outcome of a

lengthy test (probably taken on a warm day and with an oppressive headache) and various measuring processes. I am aware that I am being prepared for Life, i.e., college and a vocation. I realize that working at full potential, I am capable of doing quite well in academic processes. I appreciate that every multiple-choice-surprise quiz puts me that much nearer a Ph.D. I am grateful to the present administration for these required preparations for my benefit. However, at this time in the second semester of my junior year, I rebel at the thought of the time I waste in classes doing work that is not and cannot be relevant to my present and future existence.

What is the sense in sitting a full period in a classroom studying the obscure details of a subject in which I have grasped the "whyfores." It is depressing to realize that the teacher of a subject that might otherwise interest you, is merely filling in time until his lunch break. Why must I be subjected to a class that so utterly bores me that I find myself in a trance half the time and earning "D's?" I object to a routine of irrelevant passes at instructing pupils that inspires no thinking. I, as a free, intelligent person, wish to consider the courses that *I* will study, that *I* will learn from, that will lead to a better grasp on my concept of life and what it holds for me. This is purely self-motivated and I see no reason to be ashamed of the fact that al through my school career a series of good-enough-for-all load of boredom has been dumped on me and I see no end to it. At this point I find a future of this sort thoroughly unappetizing and a replacement to this routine a refreshing idea. I will waste no time in pulling myself out of this type of required rut in which the teachers teach as they were taught and courses are chosen for you. But still, I pity the students working their way on up through this archaic system and congratulate those who emerge with the power to think and reason and reject for themselves the shackles of a limiting school program.

Zandra was a junior in our American History class when she wrote this. Through our encouragement, we persuaded her to apply for admittance to the program for exceptional students at the local junior college, instead of spending her senior year at the high school. About six weeks into the fall semester I was jolted when I rounded a corner in the main hall and literally "ran into" Zandra.

"What are you doing here," I asked her.

"Taking a class," she replied.

"Taking a class, I don't get it? I thought you were taking classes at the junior college."

"I am, but I didn't know the district had a stupid rule that I still had to take one class here at the high school. Not only that, I'm flunking the class. I was told that I would have to take this particular English class, and honest, I know more than the teacher."

Zandra may have been stretching the truth, but I have no doubt that the material being covered in the class was an insult to her intelligence. "No good rule could be that bad."

This same thing happens time and time again in our public schools. I was sitting at my desk working on some papers that were written by students in my college class when the phone rang. At the other end was a counselor from the local high school.

"Tom, what I have to tell you surprised me as much as it will surprise you, but I know you would want to know — Kathy has cut class and we do not know why."

"Thank you for calling me. I'll take care of it when Kathy gets home tonight."

Surprised is a mild way of putting my reaction. Kathy was a 4.0 student, chosen "Girl of the Year" by the teachers and senior class. Cutting class just was not part of her behavior pattern; consequently, I knew there was a very good reason for what she did, and frankly I was not too upset about it — what did bother me was the fact that I knew she was trying to say something, but nobody at the high school was listening!

That evening, before I could even ask, Kathy said to me:

"Dad, four of us cut class today. It was such a beautiful day outside. We had all our work done and there was nothing for us to do so we went outside, sat down under a shade tree and discussed some of the concepts and issues you shared with the group of young people who met at our house the other day — you know, we were talking about the nature of being, existence and eternity. We really 'got into it' — it was better than sitting in class doing nothing."

It seems, the class had a week in which to write and turn in ten sonnets. Kathy had completed the task in three days. Instead of the teacher guiding Kathy into a challenging learning experience, she said:

"Kathy, why don't you just do the assignment over again." That was bad enough, but then she went on to her typing class where a repeat experience took place. How many times does this have to happen before a student gets "turned off," frustrated, angry, or maybe even violent?

Why should they bother going to class? What difference does it make if the school burns down? At the moment, it is not of much use to them. So what if it gets vandalized? There is little of value in it for them.

The teachers these high school students encountered tried to "teach their students as they had been taught," but it did not work. These teachers were threatened by the creative ability of their students; consequently, they did not take the time, nor put forth the effort, to challenge these inquisitive young minds.

A philosophy of education that permits a teacher to justify inadequate efforts because they are based on tradition or doctrine of long standing is not doing justice to the young people placed in their charge. Every teacher has a right to his/her particular philosophy, but as John Dewey very pointedly reminds those of us in the teaching profession, that each teacher also has an obligation to build for himself/herself an examined, critically-chosen set of values, rather than to act haphazardly and unconsciously.

After four years of teaching in a public high school, I found Dewey's words challenging every move I made in my classroom. I found this somewhat frustrating considering the fact that I was not thirty-four years old, I had three earned academic degrees, I had done extensive years of work with youth outside of public education, and acquired considerable years of experience in working with minority and disadvantaged young people. I thought these factors had prepared me well for work in a public classroom.

Dewey's admonition would not let me rest; consequently, my four years of teaching only highlighted my deficiencies and prompted me to return to graduate school in order to improve my teaching skills. I started my doctoral program in the area of counseling and guidance, but quickly shifted to educational philosophy. This change in my plans was prompted by Dr. F. Glenn Austin, chairman of the Philosophical and Social Foundations of Education Department, Arizona State University, Tempe, Arizona. The intellectual excitement he generated in me opened up a whole new vista of educational wonders. But, even more importantly, he introduced me to the principles, concepts, ideas, facts and skills that had been missing in my earlier educational training. Several incidents took place during this "educational high" that are worth mentioning.

Dr. Austin, by his own admission, did not believe in a supreme being (God) — I was an ordained Baptist minister, and yet Dr. Austin consented to be my advisor for my doctoral studies. This professional association became one of the prime topics of conversation in the graduate school. Graduate students were asking, "How could a 'Baptist preacher' possibly work with an atheistic philosopher?" The answer was simple; I had a need and Dr. Austin's patient guidance was helping me to fulfill that need; and as our relationship continued, it became evident that the study of philosophy had not fully satisfied Dr. Austin's personal needs.

During our academic journey, Dr. Austin made no attempt to convert me to his Experimentalist philosophy of education; nor did I attempt to persuade him that his life was not complete because he did not believe in a supreme being. He shared with me from his wealth of knowledge in the area of philosophy, and I shared with him the way God had worked in my life. Dr. Austin was not interested in trying to "change my mind," but, as he pointedly remarked to me one day; "Tom, I am only interested in helping you to better understand and communicate that which you already believe — I am not interested in making you a humanist or an experimentalist."

Dr. Austin was extremely successful in helping me achieve this goal. He helped me develop my own intellectual skills to the point that I know why I believe in God, but also why John Dewey's Pragmatic educational methods made more sense in a classroom than the authoritarian methods of my absolute-idealistic approach to teaching. I did not forsake my belief in God, but augmented it with Dewey's belief that men and women are capable of making wise choices provided they develop the intellectual abilities they bring into this world. Through this process, Dewey pointed out, individuals can reconstruct their own lives, and thus reconstruct society. And the best way to reconstruct one's life is by becoming responsible for one's own behavior.

The truth of this statement caused me to reflect upon my own personal philosophy, Absolute Idealism. Its limitation did not include the ideas espoused by John Dewey. This revelation confronted me with a moral dilemma. I could reject John Dewey's principles and retreat into my own beliefs in an absolute, universal God; or I could venture out and construct a rationale that included the major tenets of Dewey's Prgamatism and my own Absolute Idealism.

I responded to this challenge by researching and writing a number of papers for Dr. Austin.[21] His reaction to my paper, "Pragmatic Belief About Truth, and My Belief About Sources of Knowledge," was significant. The thesis of the paper involved my taking the Pragmatic concept of truth and tying it into my belief in an absolute being. He remarked: "It just might be possible."

This was the first phase in the "reconstructing" of my educational philosophy that eventually became identified in the graduate program at Arizona State as "Yonker's Idealistic Pragmatism."

As my studies continued under Dr. Austin's direction, I wondered if other graduates in the program were experiencing a similar exciting transformation. My curiosity prodded me into doing a piece of research that might throw some light on this subject. To my dismay, I found that, in general, there had been little change in the educational philosophy of students who were then in the graduate program.[22] And, even more alarming, most of them could neither identify or communicate the principles of their own educational philosophies.[23]

I was jolted by this realization as a result of an experience prompted by Dr. Austin. I had no more than finished the doctoral level course in educational philosophy when he suggested I take the master's level course. This seemed strange to me but I took his advice and became one of the sixty students in his class. For three weeks I never uttered a word — I just listened — but the remarks made by a high school principal from Prescott, Arizona, during the fourth session stunned me. He spent about ten minutes outlining what he called, THE educational philosophy for all of America's high schools. As he spoke, I glanced around the class. What I saw reminded me of a "mutual admiration society." Most of the heads were nodding approval as this principal poured out his personal assessment of THE philosophy that guided the destiny of our secondary schools.

There is a bit of irony in this story. He was describing, in detail, the Pragmatic philosophy of John Dewey and, in part, I could empathize with him; however, his presentation left the listener with the impression that this was the only philosophy presently operating in the public schools. After a few brief comments by other class members who strongly supported his position, I asked to be recognized by Dr. Austin. I spent about five minutes outlining three other philosophies that were also operating in the public schools. I also pointed out that these philosophies dominated the public school scene, not the Pragmatic philosophy of Dewey. The class reacted to my statements with stunned silence. A few minutes later the class took a short break. As I stood out in the hall, I was besieged by a group of my classmates berating me for my remarks. One woman was so outraged by my remarks that she said she would never come back to class — she never did!

Most of the students in this class were high school teachers, principals, and superintendents. The tragedy of this scene is the fact that most of them had already "made up their minds" before they came to class; consequently, the remarks I made in class were threatening to most of my classmates. How could someone in this class have the audacity to suggest that their beliefs about education might not be shared by other educators? To most of this group, I was expounding heresy!

My encounter with Dr. Austin the next day proved to be even more revealing. We were talking about the episode of the night before; after a few moments, I said to him: "Dr. Austin, now I know why you wanted me to take this master's level class — the comments of the students have been a real 'eye-opener' to me."

Dr. Austin responded: "Tom, there is one other thing I would like to point out to you. As you know, most of the individuals in the class are either teachers or administrators; however, what you do not know is that most of them have been trying to get into our doctoral program but they have been turned down. After last night's session, I think you understand why!"

Toward the end of my studies, one other thing happened that confirmed my conviction that an "open mind" is an asset when seeking for the truth. Dr. Austin was called back to the midwest when his brother suddenly died. Upon his return, we continued to enjoy frequent discussions of matters pertaining to philosophy; but a new element was injected into our discussions by Dr. Austin. He began asking me various things about my personal religious beliefs, particularly my belief about an absolute being. Why his sudden interest in an area that seemed to be foreign to his whole philosophy of life? I can only speculate! I had the feeling that the death of his brother had not raised some questions in his mind that heretofore had been of little concern to him, but now he was trying to venture out — as I had ventured out into his domain months earlier — into an area of man's experience (a personal relationship with God) that was completely foreign to him. Now I had something I could share with Dr. Austin; whereas, in the past, I had been the recipient of his most fertile mind.

I will be forever grateful to Dr. Austin for the help he gave me in developing my intellectual skills in the area of philosophy. These skills provided me with the tools I was seeking that would make me a better teacher. After two years of graduate studies I returned to my teaching duties at Modesto High School in Modesto, California, with the knowledge that I could make my classroom a more positive learning environment for all my students.

The school in which I taught was a large, traditionally-oriented, public high school. It purported to offer a comprehensive curriculum; but, in reality, the curriculum was centered around the college preparatory course of study which dominated most California high schools during the 1960's.[24]

My return to this school was greeted with cool acceptance — the administration was sure I would be seeking a college teaching position, rather than return to my former position as a high school teacher. Nothing could have been further from the truth! I simply had no desire to teach at the college level. I had repeatedly made this known to my superiors but, apparently, they found this difficult to accept. This unwelcome situation presented some interesting problems for me:

1. Most of the administrators simply did not want me around — for some reason I was perceived as a threat.
2. My department chairman was "scared to death" of me, even though I went out of my way to assure him that I wanted to use my new skills to help improve the depart-

ment — I was not interested in his job!
3. Most of my colleagues in the social studies department were cordial but had no desire to share with me professionally.
4. There was one exception, Manuel, the brilliant, blind teacher who taught in the room next to mine. He came into my room one day and, in despair, he said to me: "Tom, I can't teach another year the same way I have been for the past three years. Can we work together?" We developed the most beautiful team teaching relationship imaginable — this association resulted in the production of curriculum materials based on individual student abilities and needs.
5. The curriculum director for our school system avoided me "like the plague." She was responsible for ability sectioning in our district, but our professional relationship cooled when I pointed out the discriminatory nature of such a practice, especially since an extremely large portion of our Spanish-speaking students were placed in the lower ability level group.
6. I developed "contracts" and other individualized methods of instruction in an attempt to help students who had specific learning problems — this tended to cause friction in our department, especially when my grades literally destroyed the department's "bell-shaped curve" distribution for student grades.
7. Problems of a disruptive student nature developed in my colleagues' classes. I presented to the department the only solution. I said I would take the few disruptive students from each class, put them in one class and develop procedures to deal with the situation. The suggestion was turned down by the vice-principal: "We can't do that," he commented. I asked, "Why?" And he replied: "Because it has never been done before." I rest my case!

The most interesting set of circumstances involved a direct request that came to me from Dr. Corona, Superintendent of Schools for our district. In a memo dated June 11, 1968, subject: "Statement of Philosophy," he asked me if I would ". . .assist in the development of a statement of philosophy for the district. We are struggling without much success to develop some meaningful and acceptable orientation." I told the superintendent that I would be pleased to write out some suggestions and pass them on to this office. In a paper[25] that was put together for the district administrative staff, I pointed out that the ". . .present statement of philosophy for our district shows a misunderstanding regarding the related elements of an educational philosophy — there should be a direct, consistent relationship between the stated philosophical position, the educational aims of such a position, and the methods by which the aims are to be achieved."

To help the staff work out a consistent philosophy, I outlined the major educational philosophies that were presently operating in our public schools. At the end of this section I suggested that we should not get "hardening of the categories" and adopt, in total, one philosophical position, but develop our own by assessing the merits of each philosophy. By doing this, I pointed out, we could develop a consistent, workable, philosophy of education for our own district.

Along with my suggestions, I made some very pointed observations:

1. Minority groups in our community (Blacks, Chicanos) pointed out that ability sectioning was a negative form of segregation.
2. Our existing philosophical statement noted that the primary objective of public education is to help *each* student develop to his/her fullest, and thus, be able to act effectively in a democratic society. If this is true, then why, I pointed out, are most of our classrooms conducted by means of an authoritarian, dogmatic method of instruction?
3. I asked the question: are requirements made for students, or students made for requirements?
4. Does the present statement, ". . .to instill a respect for the search for truth" imply the search for all truth? Many students remarked that they had little opportunity to express openly and honestly, in many of their classes, their own views and opinions.
5. Our high school offers a comprehensive curriculum; but the

requirements each student must fulfill to receive a diploma reflect a heavy emphasis on college preparatory courses. And yet, a very small percentage of our graduates finish the first year of college — how does one justify such a curriculum?

6. I shared the existing statement of philosophy with the students in my classes. The following statements, they pointed out, sound good, but, in general, are not very valid.[26]

   a. "The aim of education is to develop a mature citizen..."

   b. "...The learning of facts is not the end of education...skill and knowledge in themselves are means to an end, the development of an effective individual (is the important consideration). A child must learn to think for himself..."

   c. "...It is essential that every child be helped by Modesto's schools to develop emotional maturity."

   d. "...it is the function of the school to help each child understand...the changing nature of his role in a dynamic society.

   e. "...instill in them (children) the realization that only as they accept the responsibilities of a democratic citizenship can they hope to enjoy its rights..."

   f. "...A good teacher must have command of the subject areas he is attempting to communicate to children, a familiarity with successful teaching techniques and procedures, an understanding of and love for children, and a dedication to the belief that an educated citizenry is the only means of insuring a continuation of our democratic way of life..."

   g. That the Modesto School District should be "governed by a written statement of policies, rules and regulations formulated cooperatively by the pupils, teachers, and administrators who are affected by them. All written policy statements should be reviewed periodically by these people..."

h. "...In its (American way of life) flexibility and adaptability is its strength. Its survival depends upon the success with which public education can meet the needs of a rapidly changing world..."

The students in my classes were perceptive to the fact that those statements made good "window dressing" for ourside observers, but, in point of fact, there was a wide gap between what we *said* and what we *did* in our high school as far as the process of education was concerned. I mentioned this to one of my respected colleagues on the staff. His responses were blunt: "Tom, don't expect teachers to necessarily practice in a classroom the ideas they express — to expect them to do otherwise would be too idealistic."[27]

Is it too idealistic? I doubt it! Let's be honest! Most teachers and administrators simply do not want to change. It is easy to *talk about* the great ideas enumerated above, but to put them into actual practice requires two things: (1) a change in attitude on the part of the teacher toward ideas, concepts, people and value systems that are different; and (2) work, the putting forth of an honest effort that will help students develop the attitudes and skills they will need to operate effectively in a democratic society.

The 1968 Kerner report on violence in America pointed out that one of the fundamental causes that produced the riots on the streets of American cities "...is the racial attitude[28] and behavior of white Americans toward black America."[29]

"Race prejudice," the report pointed out, "has shaped our history; it now threatens to affect our future."[30]

What white America has never fully understood, the report continues, but what the Negro can never forget:

is that white society is deeply implicated in the ghetto. White institutions created it, white institutions maintain it, and white society condones it.

...It is time to adopt *strategies for action* that will produce quick and visible progress. It is time to make good the promise of American democracy to all citizens — urban and rural, white and black, Spanish-surname,

American Indian, and every minority group.

Our recommendation embodies three basic principles:

1. To mount programs on a scale to the dimension of the problem.
2. To aim these programs for high impact in the immediate future in order to close the gap between promise and performance.
3. To undertake new initiatives and experiments that can change the system of failure and frustration that now dominates the ghetto and weakens our society.[31]

If we are to accomplish these things, the Commission pointed out, it will require new attitudes and understandings from all Americans as well as a change in our institutions.[32]

A change in attitude and a change in our institutions are necessary, according to the Commission, if we as a people really hope to curb the growing violence in our country. How can an institution, the public school, possibly help to bring about a change in attitude among our children and youth if it continues to follow an educational philosophy that *denies the concept of a pluralistic culture*, and perpetuates a value system dominated by a white, middle-class value system? Such a philosophy insists that the aim of education is to provide students with basically two things: (1) the great truths and knowledge of the past (the 3 R's and the classics); and (2) to transmit the cultural heritage of the past. If the "track record" of this educational philosophy is so great, then why is violence on the increase in our public schools?

This kind of an educational philosophy persists in our public schools because "teachers tend to teach as they have been taught." They say to themselves: "If it was good enough for me, it is good enough for my students."

Some teacher education programs at the college level are trying desperately to bring about a change in the attitudes of the students coming through their classes; but the minute most students step into a public classroom, too many teachers in that school attempt to mold the new student teacher in the image of the present teaching staff. The student teacher who does not conform usually has a difficult time, or does not receive favorable recommendations from his/her public school supervising teacher. How do I know? I have spent the last ten years of my life supervising student teachers; consequently, I have spent many hours in a number of different public high schools and witnessed the unconscious intimidation that is aimed at the neophyte teacher — I have also read hundreds of evaluations that have been written about our students. Not all schools, or supervising teachers are guilty of this practice, but its frequency is of such magnitude that many hours of class time are spent with our student teachers in an attempt to help them deal with the attitude that, "they must teach as their public school supervising teacher is now teaching," or they will not make it in the field of public education.

Where is there room for creative teaching, innovations, individualizing, and even more importantly, the analyzing of one's teaching performance in an educational system that claims it is "okay to teach as I have been taught?" Such an attitude has given rise to another new requirement in our teacher education program, discrimination and the educator. It is my task to take new students, and regular teachers who are seeking renewal of their certificates, through a seminar on this subject. Why should this even be necessary? Why do we need the law to tell us what we *should* be doing in our classrooms? Apparently the existing dominant philosophy of education practiced in most public schools had permitted all kinds of discriminatory practices to take place in our public classrooms.

The fact that I now am required to cover such subject matter in my class is a "slap in the face" to the teaching profession. Why do I need the law to tell me that I should treat *all* students — from handicapped to gifted — with equity, dignity and worth? I was taught this as a child and my adult behavior reflects this same simple truth. My philosophy does not permit me, as a teacher, to make value judgments about others, use "putdown" phrases in order to make me feel better, assume a superior attitude over my students, or place them in a combative climate where students of unequal ability compete for teacher-sanctioned favors and grades!

I vividly recall an incident that took place in a teacher education class I was taking at Duke University in 1955. The professor said to the class: "We do not need reformers in the teaching profession." Everyone in the class knew the remark was aimed at me. After class I went up to the professor and said:

"I know that remark was made for my benefit, but I do not consider myself a reformer and never will. There are some things, however, that are going on in public education that need to be changed, and I will do everything in my power to do just that. One of the things that needs to be changed is the 'double standard' that permits the teacher to treat students as inferiors, intellectually, emotionally, psychologically and spiritually. That's why students are verbally abused by too many teachers who do not belong in the teaching profession."

The professor responded: "Tom, you frighten me. That's why I'm not sure you should go into teaching."

"I frighten you for two reasons," I replied. "One, because I know how to communicate with young people. And two, because I can be very persuasive in dealing with them — am I right?"

"You are right, Tom."

"Then, what's the problem?" I replied. He just shook his head and walked away. His intellectual, "book-learn'in," subject matter orientation to teaching was foreign to my sensitive, caring, humanistic, spiritual approach to teaching and work with young people.

I would not discard, for one minute, the use of subject matter in the learning process; nevertheless, whenever a conflict does arise between presenting subject matter or moral and spiritual consideration in my class, I would have to support the position taken by the Educational Policies Commission of the National Education Association when it stated that ". . .there must be no question whatever as to the willingness of the school to subordinate *all* other considerations to those which concern moral (the making of wise choices) and spiritual standards."[33]

I have never come across a more absolute statement regarding any area of concern in the field of education. This statement is a reminder to all teachers that subject matter is important, but it is of little value if the individuals who possess it use it only for personal gain or destructive ends.

If the National Education Association "means what it said," then every teacher now at work in an American classroom must be willing to evaluate his/her educational philosophy in light of the value placed on both subject matter and the needs of students. It is not a question of either/or, but a fact that both must be given prime consideration if public education is to be meaningful for our children and youth. At the present time, public education seems to be vacillating between these two areas of concern. It cannot make up its mind which way to go! I say, why not go with both! If we do not, our children and youth are going to say to the adult population: "Take your educational system and 'stick it.' It is meaningless to us. What difference does it really make if we don't go to school, or if it burns down? We don't have any real stake in it. It might help to prepare us for *your* adult world, but it is not doing the job for the adult world that will be ours in the generations that come after you! Why won't you *listen* to us? If you did, then maybe the schools would truly be OURS. If they were, we would not vandalize them, nor would we give teachers a 'bad time,' because we would be denying ourselves the opportunity to develop skills, behaviors, attitudes, and values we will need to build a more productive and peaceful world than you have made for us!"

CHAPTER FOOTNOTES

[1] Some recent publications raise the question, is this practice discriminatory? See: Barbara Caufield, *Discrimination and the Oregon Educator*, Oregon Revised Statutes 342.120, July 12, 1978; Vernon F. Haubrich, Michael W. Apple, *Schooling and the Rights of Children*, National Society for Study of Education, 1975, Chapter 4, "Misuse of Psychological Knowledge;" Ronald J. Samuda, *Psychological Testing of Minorities*, Dodd Mead and Co., 1975.

[2] See: Thomas W. Yonker, *The Development of the Social Studies Curriculum in California Secondary Education From 1849 to 1964*, Dissertation, Arizona State University, June, 1966; W. O. Stanley, B. A. Smith, K. D. Benne, A. W. Anderson, *Social Foundations of Education*, The Dryden Press, Inc., New York, 1956, Chapter 4, "The Middle-Class Bias of Teachers," pp. 250-252.

[3] Jerry Pratt, TV Program, "Town Hall," KATU Channel Two, Portland, Oregon, October 21, 1979.

[4] See: Ken Ernst, *Games Students Play*, Celestial Arts Publishing,

Inc., 1972; also, Jenny Gray, *The Teacher's Survival Guide*, Fearon Publishers, 1967.

[5] See Sidney B. Simon and James A. Bellanca, *Degrading the Grading Myths: A Primer of Alternatives to Grades and Marks*, Association for Supervision and Curriculum Development, 1976. In Part II, "What Research Says About Grading," the authors came to the following conclusions: "...the traditional letter-grade system has more drawbacks and disadvantages than positive features...grading does not fulfill the four functions ascribed to it and that it can produce several undesirable motivational effects. In addition, the pressure on students to obtain good grades tends to undercut the purported beneficial effects of alternative marking approaches, when traditional and non-traditional methods coexist in the same system...finding satisfactory, workable alternatives will be difficult and may involve the restructuring of the whole curriculum around an individualized, competency-based or mastery-learning approach."

[6] See Ronald J. Samuda, *Psychological Testing of American Minorities: Issues and Consequences*, Dodd, Mead and Co., 1975. Chapter 1, "The Testing Controversy." The author points out that a number of studies were conducted during the 1960's on the effects of IQ testing: seven harmful consequences were discovered when these tests were applied to the field of education: (1) permanent classification of individuals; (2) invasion of privacy; (3) lack of confidentiality of test scores; (4) limited conceptions of intelligence and ability; (5) domination by the testers; (6) too much testing; and (7) cultural bias. . . .the belief that intelligence tests measure something innate — fixed at the moment of conception and for all time — still persists...What is absurd is to think that intelligence tests measure anything else but psychometric intelligence, or...what the individual has learned...what an intelligence-test score indicates is the quality of a pupil's performance on a number of mental tasks. It tells how well he can cope with tasks like those on the test at the time he takes the test, and it tells nothing more...Three major problems were identified when using standardized tests with minority groups: (1) tests may lack reliable differentiation in the range of minority-group scores, which tend to cluster at the lower end of the total range; (2) tests may not predict for the minority child what they predict for the white, middle-class child; and (3) test

results should be interpreted by professionally trained personnel who possess a thorough understanding of the scoiocultural background of the group being tested." pp. 13-17.

[7] *Acculturation* is the process whereby individuals reared in one culture and transferred to another take on the behavior patterns of the second society. This is often referred to as "Americanizing" culturally different individuals. See W. F. Ogburn, M. F. Nimkoff, *Sociology*, Riverside Press, 1946, pp. 383-384.

[8] The concept of *cultural pluralism* in education is an attempt to preserve and strengthen cultural differences within America. "Value premises of teachers will have to reflect multicultural ideals; multicultural curricular materials will have to be developed; interactions in classrooms will have to reflect respect for cultural differences; and classroom activities will have to be designed and implemented which will nourish such differences. Multicultural education will not result from the addition of a single or a few "multicultural" courses...Just as the entire institution of schooling was aimed at the elimination of diversity, so must the entire institution of schooling now be directed toward respecting and preserving cultural differences within the school setting." F. H. Klassen and D. M. Gollnick (eds.). *Pluralism and the American Teacher: Issues and Case Studies*, Ethnic Heritage Center for Teacher Education of the American Association of Colleges for Teacher Education, 1977, p. iii.

[9] Thomas Yonker, *The Teaching of Morality in the Public Schools*, A paper prepared for the Modesto Teachers' Association and the California Teachers' Association, 1968.

[10] Lawrence Kohlberg, *The Child As A Moral Philosopher*; James P. Shaver, William Strong, *Facing Value Decisions*; Louis E. Raths, Merrill Harmin, Sidney B. Simon, *Values and Teaching*; Virginia Hash, *Values*; Fred M. Newman, Donald W. Oliver, *Clarifying Public Controversy*; James A. Banks. *Teaching Strategies For the Social Studies, Inquiry, Valuing, Decision-Making*; Jack Frankel, *How To Teach About Values*.

[11] A Fundamentalist minister and former State Chairman of the

Oregon Republican Party.

[12]Thomas Yonker, *The Development of the Social Studies in California Secondary Education From 1849 to 1964*. A doctoral dissertation, Arizona State University, 1966. The thesis of this dissertation challenged this position and, in turn, offered some viable alternatives.

[13]The passage cited from Dr. Rafferty's book, and a critical examination of other parts of his book, reveal that he has little understanding of John Dewey's attitude toward subject matter in the public school curriculum. Dr. Rafferty gives one the impression that Dewey had little use for subject matter. On the contrary, Dewey feels subject matter does play a central role in the life of the student, but for Dewey, it should not be the center of focus in a child's learning experience. In John Dewey's book, *The Child and the Curriculum*, he points out that the main concern of the teacher "is the way in which that subject may become a part of the (child's) experience; what there is in the child's present that is usable with reference to it? how such elements are to be used; how his own knowledge of the subject matter may assist in interpreting the child's needs and doings, and determine the medium in which the child should be placed in order that his growth may be properly directed. He is concerned, not with the subject matter as such, but with the subject matter as a related factor in a total and growing experience." John Dewey, *The Child and the Curriculum*, University of Chicago Press, 1959.

[14]Max Rafferty, *Suffer Little Children*, Signet Book, 1962, p. 34.

[15]Ibid., p. 38.

[16]Max Rafferty would support Arthur Jensen's work on intelligence, which, by the way, is back in the news again as we begin the decade of the 1980's. Jensen's studies have been soundly criticized by numerous colleagues in his field, as being racist. His findings support the thesis that Blacks are inferior to Whites intellectually; however, he gives little attention to the devastating environmental factors that have plagued Blacks over the past three hundred years. Common sense dictates that any individual, Black or White, subjected to similar environmental conditions would

score lower on an intelligence test than one exempt from such conditions; however, this does not mean that the individual, the Black, is less intelligent than the one, White, who scored higher on the test.

[17] Rafferty, op.cit., p. 41.

[18] Ibid.

[19] Barbara Caulfield, *Discrimination and the Oregon Educator*, Teacher Standards and Practices Commission, State of Oregon, 1978, p. 1.

[20] Ibid., p. 2.

[21] Thomas W. Yonker, "Pragmatic Belief About Truth, and My Belief About Sources of Knowledge;" "Should Moral and Spiritual Values Be Taught In The Public Schools;" "The Problem of Identifying the Relationship Between A Philosophy of Education and Aims, Curriculum and Methods of Classroom Instruction;" "An Idealistic Philosophy of Education;" "Some Social and Educational Implications of the Writings of Rousseau, Hegel and Dewey."

[22] Thomas Yonker, "The Problem of Identifying the Relationship Between A Philosophy of Education and Aims, Curriculum and Methods of Classroom Instruction," A research paper, Arizona State University, 1960.

[23] Ibid.

[24] Thomas Yonker, *The Development of the Social Studies in California Secondary Education*, pp. 117-126.

[25] Tom Yonker, *Some Suggestions Regarding the State of Philosophy for the Modesto City Schools*, 1968.

[26] Modesto City Schools, *Proposed Modesto School District Philosophy*, 1968.

[27]Thomas Yonker, *Statement of Philosophy, Modesto High School,* April 27, 1968.

[28]Carl T. Rowan, "Inferiority Old Fight For Blacks," *Oregonian,* January 14, 1980, p. B3. In his column, Carl T. Rowan made some very pointed comments about the reappearance of Arthur Jensen's work on intelligence among blacks. In every generation, he pointed out, "they pop up, these hustlers with their pseudo-scientific evidence that black people are inherently inferior." The tragedy, Rowan exclaimed, is the fact that our society is so fascinated by that proposition, that these hustlers get a wide audience.

One of the most prominent in recent years has been Arthur Jensen. His work was given national attention in the late 1960's and early 1970's. He is now back on the American scene. In his most recent book, "he defends IQ testing against charges that such tests are culturally biased and do not measure accurately the potential of all Americans — especially blacks from deprived backgrounds."

Jensen asserts that, "There is a true difference in the general intelligence between blacks and whites, and at this time it is impossible to devise a reasonable test of mental abilities which does not show that difference."

Jensen insists — even though he admitted on a recent TV interview that we do not know what intelligence is — that black people have a lower ability to reason conceptually than white people.

Other psychologists have taken Jensen to task for ignoring or glossing over significant studies showing that school and home environment are important factors in test scores.

Rowan's observations regarding the return of Arthur Jensen were very blunt: "Common sense tells us much more than his alleged scholarship:"

1. We *know* that the average black American woman is much more likely to be malnourished during the time of pregnancy than the average white woman.
2. We *know* that black women receive far less prenatal care than white women.
3. We *know* that black babies are more likely to be born prematurely, because of deprivation, than are white babies,

and that a premature birth adds to the risk of mental retardation.

4. We *know* that black babies are more likely to have bad diets and be exposed to childhood diseases than are white children.

5. We *know* that black families must survive on $57 for every $100 available to the white family; consequently, black children are less likely than white children to be exposed to books, magazines, newspapers, cultural experiences or parental influences that make for good test scores.

"Given these and other disparities in environment and opportunity," Rowan exclaimed, "is anyone really surprised that a black ten-year-old might perform at the level of a white eight-year-old?"

"If Jensen can't understand the impact of environment on the black children of America, then we have to doubt his intelligence."

[29] U. S. Riot Commission Report, *Report On The National Advisory Commission On Civil Disorders, The New York Times*, 1968, p. 10.

[30] Ibid.

[31] Ibid., p. 2.

[32] Ibid.

[33] Educational Policies Commission, National Education Association and The American Association of School Administrators, *Moral and Spiritual Values in the Public Schools*, as found in Benjamin S. Weiss, *The Courts and the Schools*, National Educators Fellowship, Inc., p. 23.

CHAPTER VI

WHERE DO WE GO FROM HERE: SOME CONCLUSIONS AND RECOMMENDATIONS

CONCLUSIONS

1. *The highly competitive nature of our society is one of the major factors that has contributed to violence in our public schools.* Our society is highly competitive in nature and it is very doubtful if this situation is going to change in the near future. The public schools cannot ignore this fact. To do so would not only be very foolish on their part, but they would be dishonest in trying to help students cope with the culture of which they are a part.

Competition is here to stay, but for the majority of educators to propagate the assumption that competition *has to be* one of the principal factors that motivates students to learn needs careful examination. It is an important factor, but cooperation is just as important!

Arthur Combs, in his book, *Myths in Education*, points out that thousands of teachers and school administrators endorse the concept that schools should prepare young people to live in our competitive society. This statement, according to Combs, is almost totally false:

> the damage done in its name, however, is colossal. A school system that glorifies competition will, almost certainly, fail to prepare its students to live effectively in the modern world. The notion that ours is primarily a competitive society is a myth. Actually, we live in the

most cooperative, interdependent society the world has ever known.

Two great trends in human history have made cooperation an absolute must for our contemporary way of life: (1) the ever increasing dependence of people on one another, and (2) the tremendous increase of power in the hands of individuals.[1]

We laud the "free enterprise system" as the prime example of the competitive spirit that must be passed on to the young. And yet, every large industry or corporation in America — U. S. Steel, General Motors, etc. — depend upon the cooperative efforts of thousands of workers, stockholders, as well as union and management, to survive and stay in business.

It is true that we tend to glorify competition for two reasons: (1) the personal joy and excitement we experience as we witness an athletic contest; and (2) the exhilaration we personally feel when involved in some sort of competitive game. "It is not surprising that such good feelings should be translated into the belief that competition is a good and desirable aspect of life."[2] As a game, or as a means of handling scarcity or conducting a political campaign, Combs points out, competition can be useful; but as a universal way of life it leaves much to be desired and as a goal of education, it is a disaster.[3] Why? Because we live in a highly cooperative society and contemporary schools are helping students develop skills for a society which does not exist, a competitive society. A competitive society is based on the following assumptions:[4]

1. Competition can only work if people agree to seek the same goals and follow the same rules — if we want total conformity, a commitment to competition is one effective way to achieve it. Ours is a pluralistic society, composed of many subcultural groups. Maintaining self-identity among these groups has added richly to our cultural heritage — this is far from advocating cultural conformity.
2. Competition as a way of life produces the belief that, of necessity, someone must win and someone must lose in life's activities. This "dog-eat-dog attitude" is contrary to

the basic guidelines established by our forefathers for cooperative living in a democratic society. In 1953, a study was made of the three thousand young U.S. soldiers who had been held captive by the North Koreans. One thousand of them "gave in" to brainwashing, which resulted in the death of a number of their comrades while they were held captive. One of the major factors attributed to this problem was the fact that these young men, while held prisoner, talked about a "dog-eat-dog attitude and every man for himself kind of behavior...Many prisoners said that they ...were primarily concerned with their own welfare and never stopped to think, even to consider for a moment the possibility that their actions might harm others."[5] It seems that these young men "had not been taught a sense of *personal responsibility for the welfare of others.*"[6]

This study concluded that our American educational system has failed miserably in helping our young people develop the skills they need to live in our society:

> Our educational system must be directed ...not just at the goal of becoming a happy person in a comfortable country, but at becoming an active, responsible, participating member of this free society.[7]

2. *Glorifying winning at the cost of human values produces fear of other people.* There is nothing wrong with competition when practiced in proper proportion with other activities in life. But when glorifying winning (getting high grades, top honors in school, the best athlete, etc.) at the cost of human values, competition produces fear of other people. This is a direct contradiction to the kind of attitude required if a people are to maintain a successful, cooperative society.[8]

The public schools of America are charged with the responsibility of preparing the nation's youth to become effective citizens:

To meet that expectation, schools cannot afford to predicate goals and practices on false assumptions about the world they are readying students to enter. Preparing students to live and work in a complex, cooperative society requires, at the very least, such goals as the following: autonomy, responsibility, willingness to pull one's fair share of the load, concern and tolerance for others, appreciation of human values, commitment to human welfare, commitment to democratic principles, respect for the dignity and integrity of every human being, and the necessary skills and understandings to participate effectively in personal and group interaction. Such objectives do not preclude the achievement of excellence in traditional content and subject matter. They determine how such excellence will be put to use in the broader society in which students must spend the rest of their lives.[9]

3. *The highly competitive nature of our culture is reflected in the competitive activities employed by teachers in their classrooms.* When one examines the system of public education in America, it is seen at once to reflect the competitive spirit of the culture. Consequently, it should be no surprise that the competitive mode tends to dominate the atmosphere of learning in most of our public classrooms. Such an atmosphere tends to reinforce such negative behaviors as anger, fear, frustration, and violence. If this is true, then our public schools are not only contributing to the development of disruptive, violent behavior, but they are actually perpetuating such behaviors by condoning extensive competitive activities within the public classroom.

4. *The failure of teachers to share their power and authority with students has caused friction between these two groups.* It is a fact of life that the concepts *power* and *authority* operate extensively in our public schools. These concepts, in and of themselves, are not negative nor do they have to be destructive in nature. The application of these concepts, however, are often misused by educators who apply them unilaterally to

school activities that directly effect student learning and conduct. In the few cases where educators have attempted to share their power and authority with students, student disruptive behavior tends to be minimal.

Various reports published during 1979 and 1980 tend to support the need for having students become more involved in the process of establishing rules and regulations that govern student behavior. A report on the *Prevention of School Violence and Vandalism* by Senator Birch Bayh's Juvenile Delinquency Subcommittee recommended that schools should educate students regarding their rights and responsibilities and "involve them in the process of establishing written codes for the school community."[10]

This report recognized that such steps take extra time and effort, on the part of school staff, but it emphasized that broad student participation in developing and revising school rules is one of the most beneficial activities in which students can take part.[11]

Similarly, a research report by Johns Hopkins University suggests that students' participation in the school decision-making process "often increases student commitment to the school and can reduce student offenses against teachers and the school."[12] Also, a study conducted by Cynthia Kelly in the Chicago area, indicated that in those schools "which more carefully observe the letter and spirit of the Constitution concerning students' due process rights, students tended to have a more positive attitude toward school rules, be more positive about the law, and be more positive about their learning."[13]

Research on this issue is incomplete, but recent data seems to indicate that schools which allow students "freedom of expression tend to be more effective in preparing them to be active, responsible citizens than those that emphasize rigid discipline and unquestioning compliance."[14] In schools where rigid discipline is stressed, students feel powerless, consequently, they become frustrated with "the system" and often vent their frustration through some form of disruptive behavior.

5. *Students' rights have been increased in recent years due to the court's interpretation of the in loco parentis and due process legal concepts.* The courts, during the decades of the 1960's and 1970's, granted more rights to students than at any time in the history of public educa-

tion. Until this period of time public school educators exercised almost complete authority over the lives of students. Teachers and administrators used the legal concept, in loco parentis, to support their right to exercise such authority. But litigation brought against the public schools in the 1960's pointed out three things: (1) historically, educators had been using this concept to maintain complete authority over the lives of students while in school; (2) the intent of this legal concept was to limit such authority to the area of student life, referred to as discipline; and (3) the misuse of this legal concept by public school people has created a great deal of frustration on the part of students, thus precipitating a great deal of unnecessary confrontation between school officials and students.

This confrontation, in the 1960's, prompted the courts, in the 1970's, to extend the legal doctrine of due process to children and youth. Heretofore, the doctrine had been reserved, primarily, for adults who were seeking help from the courts. Once this legal process was extended to the child-youth population, many school officials felt their authority was being eroded and, thus, their effectiveness in dealing with students was in jeopardy. On the other hand, students felt they were merely asking for specific rights and privileges which were guaranteed to them by the supreme law of the land, The Constitution.

6. *The criterion of love can better cope with the problem of violence than the authoritarian criterion that presently dominates the public schools.* Criteria, to cope with violence in our public schools, established under the umbrella of the traditional, authoritarian philosophy of education that is practiced in most of our public schools has not worked; consequently, a new approach to this problem is mandatory if a solution is to be found. The criterion of love, when broken down into specific behaviors — patience, forgiveness, being constructive, "going the extra mile," treat others as you would like to be treated — is recommended as the standard of behavior for teachers if they really hope to curb violent behavior in their classrooms.

Contrary to popular opinion — the notion that rigid, disciplined behavior and not love should be the factor that controls students' actions in a classroom — historical evidence does support the position that the behavior, love, can be a very effective, positive force against those who would use violence to achieve their goals. Gandhi forced the British out of India by using the process of passive resistance. Martin Luther King, Jr. used the same tactic to bring about better living conditions for Blacks in the South. And the Friends (Quakers) have, throughout their history, consistently used the same approach when their people have been confronted with taking an active part in the various wars our country has engaged in over the past two centuries. Also, the few teachers who have applied the concept of love to their teaching methods have experienced little, if any, problem with disruptive student behavior in their classrooms.

7. *Poor mental health of some teachers is a significant factor that has directly contributed to violence in the classroom.* It is most difficult, if not impossible, to prove a cause-effect relationship when one is confronted with a large social problem such as violent student behavior that has had a most disrupting effect upon the learning environment of the public classroom. There is enough extant evidence to support the contention that the poor mental health of some (too many) public school teachers is one factor that has directly contributed to this problem. At the present time, close to three million students are daily placed in the care of adult teachers whose mental health, at best, can be classified as poor. Students under their care are abused in a number of ways; the most direct being verbal abuse. Teachers who make use of such behaviors cause anger and frustration in their students who, in turn, tend to vent their anger through some form of violent behavior that might be aimed directly at the teacher or it might result in some form of vandalized attack upon the school.

8. *A few public schools in the United States have been successful in eliminating violence in their schools by making use of non-traditional teaching methods in their classrooms.* There are a few schools scattered around the country where school officials have attempted to deal with the student who feels alienated from their public school experiences. These schools have been very successful in bringing such students back into the "mainstream" of education for the following reasons: (1) teachers working with this kind of student were *exceptional* teachers; (2) these teachers shunned the teaching methods that are commonly used in the typical

public school classroom; (3) these teachers produced learning materials and activities that developed a warm, intimate relationship with students; (4) teachers working with delinquent youth developed individualized teaching materials that permitted the youth to proceed at a rate of speed commensurate with their academic abilities and skills; (5) the willingness of teachers to work on a one-to-one basis with students as well as in small group sessions; (6) students have an opportunity to choose from a number of different options which helps the student develop self-reliance as well as skills that fit his/her individual needs, abilities, and interests; and (7) the system of learning established for these young people is success oriented — "success is the name of the game."

9. *Getting rid of tenured teachers whose behavior reflects poor mental health is almost impossible.* Getting rid of an experienced teacher who might have mental health problems is most difficult for the following reasons: (1) it is difficult to find public school administrators who are qualified to evaluate the performance of a classroom teacher; (2) administrators do not have the time to do an adequate job of evaluating teachers; (3) a qualified administrator might be reluctant to evaluate teachers because of the political problems involved; (4) it is easier for an administrator to give blanket notice of acceptance to all teachers than to concern himself/herself with the mountain of paperwork involved in the evaluative process; (5) most states do not require administrators to make observations of tenured teachers; and (6) most states have not developed job descriptions and performance standards on which teachers are to be evaluated.

10. *Teachers tend to teach as they have been taught.* It is easier to accept established doctrines, traditional customs and behaviors, than it is to take the time and effort to critically examine them, test them out, and then form one's own conclusions based on one's evaluative efforts. Most public school teachers in America have not bothered to put themselves through such a rigorous, reflective process; consequently, most of our teachers have rejected any philosophy that is reflective in nature (Pragmatism), and unconsciously adopted a philosophy that is either regressive

(Perennialism) in nature, or one that supports the "status quo" (Essentialism).

About 80% of the public schools in America are dominated by the latter two philosophies. The assumptions, doctrines, principles and concepts inherent in these two educational philosophies have produced the following two situations in our public schools: (1) the schools tend to be run in a very authoritarian manner; and (2) most teachers employ indoctrination as the principle method of instruction in their classes.

These two factors have helped to produce the following negative practices, behaviors and attitudes in our public schools: (1) the tracking of students that has led to discriminatory practices, especially among minority students; (2) students who are not willing to accept the responsibility for their own behavior; (3) extensive use of "verbal intimidation" by school staff to keep students "in line;" (4) the propagation of the "superior/inferior" attitude on the part of teachers; and (5) the strong effort to maintain the "status quo" by reinforcing conforming behavior, insisting intelligence is a fixed attribute that can be supported by standardized tests and acculturating minority students by treating them as a part of a "melting pot" society and not a pluralistic society.

11. *The factors of fear, threat, negative teacher attitudes, bored students and the power struggle between students and school staff have directly contributed to disruptive behavior in the classroom.* The following five factors have had a negative effect upon the learning environment of the public schools:

(1) *Fear*: Some teachers tend to confuse the two terms *fear* and *respect*. Respect one earns and as the students and teacher develop a feeling of mutual respect, fear diminishes in the classroom. This begins to happen when the teacher treats students with dignity and worth.

(2) *Threat*: If a teacher hopes to have positive learning experiences in his/her classroom, all forms of threat must be eliminated from the classroom environment. The best way for a teacher to do this is to remember that students become threatened when they are involved in a situation with

which they cannot cope — help them to "find a way out."
- (3) *Negative teacher attitudes*: Teachers can avoid this problem by learning to *communicate* with students, developing the skill of *acceptance* and by eliminating "put downs" in their classrooms.
- (4) *Bored students*: Most students become bored because their teachers do not enjoy teaching, project a superior attitude toward the students, use the same "old methods" of presenting material to the class, do not involve students in the learning process, and do not make the material relevant to the needs of students.
- (5) *Power struggle*: During the 1960's and 1970's student demands for more autonomy over their lives clashed with "hold-the-line" educators who felt students had very limited right to voice an opinion in such matters.

12. *The teacher's philosophy of education is going to determine the methods of instruction employed by him/her to conduct learning activities in his/her classroom*. Most teachers who adhere to the basic principles of either the Perennialistic or Essentialistic philosophies of education will *tend* to use authoritarian methods of instruction in their classrooms. On the other hand, most teachers who have developed a philosophy of education that incorporated the basic concepts of the Pragmatic philosophy are more likely to use democratic, or more flexible methods of instruction in their classrooms. The latter philosophy is more conducive to meeting the individual needs of students; consequently, teachers who tend to employ methods of instruction based on Pragmatic assumptions are less likely to have problems of disruptive behavior in their classes for the following reasons: (1) alternatives are presented to students which given them a chance to make curricular choices that fit their abilities; skills, interests and needs; (2) individualized instruction would be stressed, thus permitting the possibility for greater academic success based on the student's ability to move at his/her own pace; (3) process (means) will be stressed, thus the students will have many opportunities to develop their problem-solving skills; (4) subject matter will be important, but it will be used as a reservoir of information by students for the purpose of solving their own

problems, not as a body of irrelevant information to be memorized because the teacher thinks it is important; (5) students will be permitted to "draw their own conclusions," based on the results of their reflective consideration of all factual information that was part of the "reservoir" made available to all students; and (6) students will be so *actively* involved in the process of learning that they will have little opportunity to "get into mischief."

13. *The individuals who direct, supervise and administer the public schools are spending more time dealing with the symptoms than the causes of violence in our public schools.* Example: principals and administrators spend more time dealing with student behavior problems (symptoms) than they do with teachers who threaten or abuse students (causes). School officials find it much easier to reprimand a student or remove him/her from a classroom (or the school) than to take the time and effort to deal with the causes that precipitated his/her disruptive behavior. Consequently, most disruptive students rarely are exposed to positive experiences within the school setting that modify or eliminate undesirable behavior.

14. *Violence is a learned behavior, and since it is learned, it can be changed, altered or eliminated.* Not much effort is put forth by the public schools to do this for three reasons: (1) the cost in time and effort is too great; (2) the basic philosphy of our schools is to teach subject matter and the basic elements of our cultural heritage, not to get involved in the "life adjustment" problems of students; and (3) the vast majority of young people coming out of our teacher preparation programs are well versed in the teaching of their subject matter but woefully unprepared to cope with student behavior problems.

15. *The existence and perpetuating of a "double standard" in the public schools has caused many students to lose respect for the teacher model who stands in the front of the class each day and says: "Don't do as I do, do as I say." — students aren't buying this any more.* Example: students

ask the "powers that be;" "If teachers can smoke, swear, etc., then why can't we?"

The historical image of the public school teacher was one who set a "good example" for the student. Contemporary teachers have tended to reject this notion and instead have replaced it with a curious, self-centered concept of adulthood: "Since I am an adult, I can do what I please and you (the student) had better do what I say or else!" Is it any wonder that students are being "turned off" by the teachers who set this kind of an example?

A study was released in June, 1980, by a research group within the California State Department of Education regarding school dropouts. The report pointed out that student dropouts in California were three times the national average — students were not dropping out in order to work, simply because jobs were not available. I terminated by public school teaching in California in 1970; at that time this problem already existed. Question: Why did it take the State of California ten years to recognize the fact that they had a problem?

RECOMMENDATIONS

ADMINISTRATIVE

Every administrator who is in charge of a public school should take a serious look at the philosophy of education that serves as the foundation for all learning experiences that take place within his/her school. If the school is having problems with violent behavior, an assessment might be made to determine if the approach to learning has become so rigid and/or authoritarian that it is "turning off" the students — this is not too difficult to do. The following suggestions might be helpful:

1. Are rules so rigid that students have very few choices; or do administrators and teachers find it difficult to deal with "exceptions" when they arise?
2. Requirements form the core of most learning experiences

within a school, but the curriculum should be flexible enough to meet the needs of *all* students, especially the exceptional student (handicapped, minority, gifted, etc.).
3. A self-study by the staff might help identify some negative teacher procedures that they are using in their classrooms — they might be totally unaware that such is the case. If the self-study included the entire staff, it could deter embarrassment on the part of the individual offending teacher.
4. School districts could develop guidelines that permitted alternative credential approaches that allowed a student *early* or *late* completion of all requirements for graduation.
5. Professional training should be provided for administrators who are responsible for the supervision and evaluation of the teaching staff. Once the training has been completed, the school district should provide the administrator with the time to supervise and evaluate adequately all of his/her teaching staff on a regular basis. Teachers who are "turning off" students could then be given help to improve their teaching performance.

School districts could also provide in-service training sessions for their teaching staff, administrators and school board members. The purpose of these sessions would be to provide a positive learning environment where the participants could become involved in the following activities:

1. Sharing activities that would help teachers, in particular, become more perceptive to the fact that the teaching-learning process is more a function of *sharing* than the "impartation of absolute knowledge."
2. Discussions and "give and take" sessions that could help teachers re-define their "power" role within the classroom.
3. Small group sessions where board members and administrators could explore such concepts as power, authority, freedom, due process, in loco parentis, etc.
4. Large group sessions where legal experts could provide legal information regarding discrimination in the classroom, the rights and responsibilities of students and all school

staff.

Institutions of higher learning who are involved in preparing young men and women for the teaching profession should make the following changes in their programs:

1. Increase the length of the training program at least one year.
2. Increase the exposure of their students to the basic philosophical, psychological and sociological principles which govern human thinking, behaving and relationships.
3. Increase the exposure of their students to the problems of cultural and ethnic minorities and the handicapped.
4. Require that each student demonstrate, in a classroom environment, that he/she can cope effectively with *all* types of students under normal as well as "explosive" situations.
5. Require that each student in the program serve one year as an intern under the combined direction of a college and public school supervisor. At the end of the internship, his/her performance would be evaluated. At least part of the evaluation would be based on the intern's ability to cope with the following:
    (1) Help all students develop a positive self-concept.
    (2) Treat all students with dignity and worth.
    (3) Listen to a student who wants to discuss a problem.
    (4) Communicate with all students regardless of ability, attitude toward school or value system.
    (5) Teach subject matter content using positive reinforcement.
    (6) Use individual teaching methods (contracts, LAPS, etc.), when they are appropriate.
    (7) Exhibit a sense of humor, especially in times of stress.
    (8) Exhibit patience and understanding, particularly when dealing with troubled students.

(9) Demonstrate the he/she can "defuse" a potentially explosive situation in the classroom.

TEACHERS

Changing the self-concept of the student is hard enough but changing the self-concept of the teacher is even more difficult. Consequently, two things are needed to deal with this problem: (1) a longer period of time for the training of prospective teachers; and (2) valid, continuing education for individuals now working in our public schools. School districts could make available the following professional experiences in the hope that they might help the teaching staff develop the attitudes, behaviors and skills they need to cope with violent student behavior:

1. Provide in-service training sessions during the school year for the purpose of helping the staff evaluate their personal self-concept, philosophy of life and educational philosophy.
2. Provide sensitivity (controlled) sessions which would help the staff "come to grips" with their own feelings, emotions, beliefs and behaviors.
3. Provide frequent small group "bull sessions" in which staff members could "get things off their chests," without threat of retaliation from the administration, colleagues, students, or parents.
4. Provide reading and writing workshops for teachers who work in specific subject matter areas. Teachers could develop their own skills and materials that would be used in their subject matter areas to help students improve their ability to read and write. This would help to eliminate the "back to basics" critics that have sounded the alarm that contemporary young people do not know how to read and write.
5. Teachers should learn the relaxation techniques (autogenics, biofeedback, etc.) which doctors have found so successful in treating patients who are under stress or experiencing a great deal of pain.[15] These techniques could be

used in two ways: (1) the teacher could use the skills to reduce his/her own level of stress and thus have a calming effect upon the class; or (2) the techniques could be used in order to "calm down" a disorderly class, group of students or an individual who is "getting uptight."

6. Dr. Martin Luther King, Jr. carried on a very successful non-violent movement that resulted in many positive changes for the Black people in the South. His movement was influenced by the principle of Gandhi's "passive resistance" philosophy. This philosophy, in essence, rejects forceful or violent behavior as a valid means of achieving goals or ends. Consequently, any group or individual who became a follower of King rejected violence as a means of bringing about positive social change for Blacks.

One of the reasons King was able to improve living and working conditions for Southern Blacks was due to the fact that his followers had learned to meet force, not with more force but with non-violent behavior. They had learned a very specific technique that required King's followers to behave in a positive way toward those who would even destroy them. The technique involved exposure to the following types of behaviors: (1) abusive language; (2) being spat upon; (3) attacks by leashed dogs; and (4) just about every type of negative behavior contrived by man.

Exposure to these types of behaviors taught King's followers that the behavior of their enemies was not going to control their behavior; consequently, as Dr. King put it, "Do to us what you will but we will still love you."

Similar techniques could be used to train teachers how to combat disruptive or violent behavior. The results of such training would be twofold: (1) some teachers would develop the skills to handle all forms of disruptive behavior that might be thrown at them; or (2) some teachers would be so repulsed by such techniques that it would "turn them off," thus indicating that they should not be placed in classrooms where possible explosive situations might occur.

7. Professional training could be provided for selective master teachers who are interested in providing supervision for their colleagues – this could help teachers identify the areas of weakness in their teaching area and thus provide data for improvement.
8. In-service curriculum experiences could be set up to help teachers do three things: (1) develop individualized teaching materials that can be adapted to the ability, needs and interests of the student; (2) develop guidelines that permit the teacher to share his/her authority with students regarding the running of the classroom; and (3) develop procedures and skills whereby students can act as tutors and/or teachers for students who are having difficulty in the class.
9. The school district should provide experiences (one day, weekend or extended camps) where teachers are directly exposed to children and youth who have problems that are related to school life. The interaction between the adults (teachers) and students could help the teachers do the following things: (1) "check out" their own personal feelings, both positive and negative, when it comes to working with students who are discipline problems; (2) teachers would soon learn if they had the emotional and psychological "guts" to cope with problem students; and (3) develop attitudes, skills and techniques that would help them to cope with disruptive student behavior.
10. In-service training programs in behavior modification techniques could be offered to the teaching staff at various times throughout the school year. Such programs should include the following elements: (1) an explanation and discussion of the principles and concepts which support the rationale for the technique; (2) an evaluation of each participant's progress in order to insure a full understanding of these principles and concepts; (3) a practical demonstration, by the instructor, of the application of these principles; and (4) an opportunity for each participant to demonstrate that he/she can use these principles effectively.

STUDENTS

Educators tend to give "lip service" to the concept of individual differences when it comes to matters of classroom teaching methods. A great deal is inferred that each child or young person is a very unique individual. But when "push" comes to "shove" the actual methods employed by most public school teachers do not support the concept that those placed in their charge are unique individuals — no wonder so many young people are "turned off" by events that take place in their classes. The following recommendations might help to reduce student frustration and thus reduce the incidents of violence within the classroom:

1. Develop labs (reading, writing, study skills, research, etc.) which will help meet specific needs of any student who is disadvantaged or handicapped in any way. These labs could help such students work at their own ability levels.
2. Teachers who work in specific subject matter areas could develop individual learning contracts with their students. If this is not feasible, at least it could be done with problem students or students who have exceptional ability. Under the contract system, the student knows exactly what is expected of him/her, thus the student takes charge of his/her own life. This tends to minimize negative confrontations between teacher and student.
3. All students should be carefully screened by counselors and identified as being either "head" or "hand" oriented regarding their abilities to cope with academic work. The "head" student could then be matched with those teachers whose emotional and intellectual makeup works best with students in "secondary" relationships and have the ability to work well with abstractions; the "hand" student would be placed with teachers who work well in "primary" relationships and have the patience to work with students who are good at using their hands.
4. The misuse of "power" and "authority" by adult educators have rendered students powerless, thus causing them to rebel. This situation can be improved in a very simple way —

by inviting students to become a part of the power structure within the school system. Ramapo High School in Spring Valley, New York, set up guidelines in 1969 which made this possible.[16] The principal of the school remarked: "We've seen a miracle. Last year the student body and faculty. . .were so far apart that they were screaming at each other. At one mass meeting, some kids seized the stage. Today the leaders of those kids are deeply involved in the school administration."[17]

"In effect," Assistant Superintendent Sugarman pointed out, "we've told the students we respect you. We value you. We have faith in you. We need your help. Once you take that attitude all sorts of things fall into place."[18]

Nancy Brown, a senior at Ramapo, remarked: "I'm a responsible citizen of this school and it's right and proper that I have an equal voice with the teachers. But, notice I said *responsible*. We kids have no right to go off in some silly direction."[19]

Howard Jacobs, the school principal, has no doubts that SFAC (Student-Faculty-Administration Council) will work, even though he received many phone calls from other principals asking how he "dared to surrender a principal's absolute power to democratic voting."[20] He said if he was transferred to another school, the first thing he would do would be to set up a Student-Faculty-Administrative Council.[21]

The Ramapo experience is not the only way the adult school staff can share its power and authority. The basic principle that should guide such efforts is simply, as students become more responsible, they receive more privileges. But, students can only become more responsible if they are given opportunities to do so. Here are some suggested ways this may be accomplished:

(1) Establish a student government that is patterned after the supreme law of the land, the Constitution.
(2) Establish a student judicial council that has the power to deal with student disruptive behavior —

peer group pressure is far more effective than adult group pressure.
- (3) Place students on the school board and give them voting power.
- (4) Have students become directly involved with teaching by having them help in the development of curriculum materials.
- (5) Make effective use of students as teacher's aides.
- (6) Help teachers develop guidelines that permit them to operate democratic classrooms.
- (7) Develop within the educational code of the district, guidelines that support teachers who use democratic principles within their classes.
- (8) Develop school district guidelines that invite the help and participation of *all* segments of the community, particularly those parts of the minority community who are not part of the power structure within the community.

CHAPTER FOOTNOTES

[1] Arthur Combs, *Myths in Education*. Allyn and Bacon, Inc., Boston, 1979, p. 15.

[2] Ibid., p. 18.

[3] Ibid.

[4] Ibid., p. 19.

[5] Major William E. Mayer, U. S. Army Psychiatrist, as interviewed in *U. S. News and World Report*, February 24, 1956, pp. 58-59.

[6] Ibid.

[7] Ibid.

[8] Combs, op.cit., p. 19.

[9] Ibid., pp. 19-20.

[10] *Update, On Law-Related Education*, Spring, 1980, p. 25.

[11] Ibid.

[12] Ibid.

[13] Ibid.

[14] Ibid.

[15] I had the privilege of spending two weeks in the Northwest Pain Center in Portland, Oregon, where I was taught specific skills that helped me to cope with severe back pain and headaches. The techniques and skills I learned at the Pain Center I now share with the students who come through the teacher training program at Linfield College.

[16] John C. Rogers, "Student Power Can Work," *Parade*, May 3, 1969, p. 8.

[17] Ibid.

[18] Ibid.

[19] Ibid.

[20] Ibid., p. 9.

[21] Ibid.

BIBLIOGRAPHY

Banks, James A. and Jean N. Grambs, *Black Self-Concept*, NY: McGraw-Hill, 1972.

Banks, James A. and Ambrose A. Clegg, Jr., *Teaching Strategies for the Social Studies: Inquiry, Valuing and Decision-Making*, second edition, Reading, Mass.: Addison-Wesley, 1977.

Barnhart, Lawrence L. (ed.), *The American College Dictionary*, NY: Harper and Brothers, 1950.

Bolmier, Edward C., *Legality of Student Disciplinary Practices*, Charlottesville, Virginia: The Michie Co., 1976.

Bolmier, Edward C., *Judicial Excerpts Governing Students and Teacher*, Charlottesville, Virginia, The Michie Company, 1977.

Brameld, Theodore, *Patterns of Educational Philosophy: Divergence and Convergence in Culturalogical Perspective*, NY: Holt, Rinehart & Winston, 1971.

Caufield, Barbara, *Discrimination and the Oregon Educator*, Salem, OR: Teacher Standards and Practices Commission, 1978.

Christian Science Monitor, "Editorial, Report of the National Commission on the Causes and Prevention of Violence," Feb. 2, 1969.

Christian Science Monitor, "Violence is as American as Cherry Pie," by

David Holstrom, July 7, 1969.

Collins, Huntly, "Teacher Evaluations Far From Adequate," **The Oregonian,** Feb. 2, 1980, Portland, Oregon.

Combs, Arthur, *Myths in Education*, Boston: Allyn & Bacon, Inc., 1979.

Combs, Arthur and others, *The Professional Education of Teachers*, Boston: Allyn & Bacon, Inc., 1974.

Dewey, John, *Seventh Yearbook, John Dewey Society*, as found in the *Elementary School Principal Journal*, Sept. 1947.

Dewey, John, *The Child and the Curriculum*, Chicago: University of Chicago Press, 1959.

Educational Policies Commission, National Education Association and the American Association of School Administrators, "Moral and Spiritual Values in the Public Schools," as found in Benjamin S. Weiss, *The Courts and the Schools*, South Pasadena, California: National Educators Fellowship, Inc.

Ernst, Ken, *Games Students Play*, Millbrae, CA: Celestial Arts Publishing Co., 1972.

Frankel, Jack R., *How To Teach About Values: An Analytic Approach*, Englewood Cliffs, NJ: Prentice-Hall, 1977.

Gray, Jenny, *The Teacher's Survival Guide*, Palo Alto, CA: Fearon Publishers, 1967.

Hash, Virginia, *Values: Awareness, Significance and Action*, Dubuque, IA: Kendall/Hung, 1975.

Haubrich, Vernon F. and Michael W. Apple, *Schooling and the Rights of Children*, National Society for the Study of Education, Berkeley, CA: McCutcheon Publishing Co., 1975.

James, Howard, *Children in Trouble: A National Scandal*, Boston: Christian Science Publishing Society, 1969.

King, Martin Luther, Jr., Address delivered before the Episcopal Society for Cultural and Racial Unity at the Episcopal Church's General Convention in St. Louis, Missouri, 1964.

Klassen, F. H. and D. M. Gollnick (eds.), *Pluralism and the American Teacher: Issues and Case Studies*, Washington, D.C.: Ethnic Heritage Center for Teacher Education of the American Association of Colleges for Teacher Education, 1977.

Kohlberg, Lawrence and Phillip Whitten, "Understanding the Hidden Curriculum: Values and Morals," *Annual Editions: Readings in Education*, Guilford, Connecticut: Dushkin Pub. Group, Inc. 1975-1976.

Mayer, Major William E., "Why Did Many GI Captives Cave In," *U. S. News and World Report*, Feb. 24, 1956.

Modesto City Schools, *Proposed Modesto School District Philosophy*, Modesto, CA, 1968.

Montagu, Ashley, "The Awesome Power of Human Love," condensed from the *Humanization of Man*, and reprinted in *Reader's Digest*, July, 1971.

Newman, Fred M. and Donald W. Oliver, *Clarifying Public Controversy: An Approach to Teaching Social Studies*, Boston: Little, Brown & Co., 1970.

Now I Have Known Me, Report on Mental Health of Cooperative Urban Teacher Education Program, Mid-Continent Regional Educational Laboratory, Kansas City, MO, Spring, 1970, Vol. I, No. 4.

Ogburn, William F. and Meyer F. Nimkoff, *Sociology*, NY: Houghton Mifflin, 1946.

Pratt, Jerry, "Town Hall," KATU-TV, Channel Two, Portland, OR, Oct. 21, 1979.

Rafferty, Max, *Suffer Little Children*, NY: Signet Books, 1962.

Raths, Louis E., Merrill Harmin, Sidney B. Simon, *Values and Teaching*, second edition, Columbus, OH: Charles E. Merrill, 1978.

Revelle, Dorothy M., Speeches presented to Shoreline Schools, September and November, 1971.

Rogers, John C., "Student Power Can Work," *Parade*, May 3, 1968.

Rowan, Carl T., "Inferiority Old Fight For Blacks," *The Oregonian*, January 14, 1980.

Samuda, Ronald J., *Psychological Testing of Minorities*, NY: Dodd Mead, 1975.

Shaver, James P. and William Strong, *Facing Value Decisions: Rationale Building for Teachers*, Belmont, CA: Wadsworth, 1976.

Simon, Sidney B. and James A. Bellanca, *Degrading the Grading Myth: A Primer of Alternatives to Grades and Marks*, Washington, D.C.: Association for Supervision and Curriculum Development, 1976.

Update, On Law-Related Education, Spring, 1980.

U. S. Riot Commission, *Report on the National Advisory Commission on Civil Disorders*, NY: The New York Times Co., 1968.

Werthan, F., *Time Magazine*, "Violence in America," July 28, 1967.

Yonker, Thomas W., *The Development of the Social Studies Curriculum in California Secondary Education, From 1849 to 1964*. Doctoral dissertation, Arizona State University, Tempe, AZ, 1966.

Yonker, Thomas W., *The Teaching of Morality in the Public Schools*, A paper parepared for the Modesto Teachers' Association and the California Teachers' Association, 1968.

Yonker, Thomas W., *The Problem of Identifying the Relationship Between A Philosophy of Education, Aims, Curriculum and Methods of Classroom Instruction* A research paper, Arizona State University, Tempe, AZ, 1960.

Yonker, Thomas W. *Some Suggestions Regarding the Statement of Philosophy For the Modesto City Schools*, Modesto High School, Modesto, CA, 1968.

Yonker, Thomas W., *Statement of Philosophy, Modesto High School*, Modesto High School, Modesto, California, April 27, 1968.